THINK

BIG

Overcoming Obstacles with Optimism

Jennifer Arnold, MD, and Bill Klein

HOWARD BOOKS
An Imprint of Simon & Schuster, Inc.
New York   Nashville   London   Toronto   Sydney   New Delhi

Howard Books
An Imprint of Simon & Schuster, Inc.
1230 Avenue of the Americas
New York, NY 10020

First Howard Books trade paperback edition January 2017

HOWARD and colophon are trademarks of Simon & Schuster, Inc.

For information about special discounts for bulk purchases, please contact
Simon & Schuster Special Sales at 1-866-506-1949 or business@simonandschuster.com.

The Simon & Schuster Speakers Bureau can bring authors to your live event. For more
information or to book an event, contact the Simon & Schuster Speakers Bureau
at 1-866-248-3049 or visit our website at www.simonspeakers.com.

Interior design by Davina Mock-Maniscalco

Manufactured in the United States of America

10 9 8 7 6 5 4 3 2 1

The Library of Congress has cataloged the hardcover edition as follows:

Names: Arnold, Jennifer, 1974– author. | Klein, Bill, 1974– author.
Title: Think big : overcoming obstacles with optimism / Jennifer Arnold and Bill Klein.
Description: First Howard Books hardcover edition. | New York : Howard Books, 2016.
Identifiers: LCCN 2016002976 | ISBN 9781501139277 (hardback)
Subjects: LCSH: Arnold, Jennifer, 1974– | Klein, Bill, 1974– | Television personalities—
United States—Biography. | Conduct of life. | Motivation
(Psychology) | BISAC: BIOGRAPHY & AUTOBIOGRAPHY / Rich & Famous. |
SELF-HELP / Motivational & Inspirational.
Classification: LCC PN1992.4.A74 A3 2016 | DDC 791.4502/8092—dc23
LC record available at http://lccn.loc.gov/2016002976

ISBN 978-1-5011-3927-7
ISBN 978-1-5011-3939-0 (pbk)
ISBN 978-1-5011-3932-1 (ebook)

To Will & Zoey,
We hope these words help you to be as big as you want to be.
Love, Mom & Dad

CONTENTS

THINK
BIG

INTRODUCTION

Each of us is stronger than we realize. Strength is something we often find in desperate moments. Often, it's those we love who end up showing us what it looks like. This happened one October Monday in 2013, when my wife, Jennifer, taught me the very definition of bravery.

I stood in a house that felt large and lifeless. And while our three-year-old son ran around playing with his toys, our two-year-old daughter wailed next to the front door. I had just introduced Zoey to her new home for the first time, but she didn't want anything to do with it, and she didn't want to be near her new daddy. Now that it was just the three of us, poor little Zoey seemed to feel like she was in some kind of prison.

After the long trip home from New Delhi, India, where we adopted Zoey, I felt like I could barely walk, yet I knew I needed to keep on going. A twenty-four-hour journey is difficult enough, but a twenty-four-hour journey with two toddlers was another experience altogether. We had embarked on it without Mommy. Jen had unfortunately been sent on her own journey—one far more difficult than mine.

While we were in New Delhi becoming acquainted with our beautiful new girl, Jen had had a medical emergency and was forced to fly back to the States a few days early. I had to bring Will and our little girl home alone.

Zoey had bonded with Jen, but not with me, and without her new mommy, she was inconsolable. Trying to soothe Zoey only made things worse. Her cries echoed throughout the house. She was in a new, strange place, with people she didn't know. The attachment that was forged in India with Jennifer was waning and her tendency to gravitate toward any female in the room made my role as her parent that much more difficult. I felt helpless and alone, as I had no real means of communicating with her. Zoey obviously wanted and needed her mother.

She wasn't the only one missing Jen.

I had to shake off the worry and the fear surrounding Jen's diagnosis. She had come back home from India and undergone immediate testing, the results of which revealed that she had a rare form of cancer, an aggressive choriocarcinoma. Since she had been treated with intensive chemo, Jen's immune system was paying the price. This meant she could not be in the house with us when we first arrived. Who knew what germs and viruses we might have picked up on that long flight back home? Jen was staying with her parents nearby.

The first thing I did after we arrived home was to call her to let her know we'd made it. We didn't talk for long. The camera crew for our TV show, *The Little Couple*, wanted to capture our arrival home. They had been with us on the journey to India, and had been there when we met Zoey for the first time. Now they wanted to catch her first reaction to seeing her new home. Our exhaustion tempered any kind of initial reaction, though, and after documenting the otherwise anticlimactic arrival home, we said our good-byes to the crew. Kate, our nanny, who'd stayed with me throughout the trip, helped us get settled, and then she, too, departed to get some rest.

Once alone with the kids, I ignored my tired body and went about getting the kids settled, fed, and to bed for some rest. Those things had to get done. I'd have to battle my exhaustion along with Zoey's exasperation.

A knock on the back door got my attention and made me mutter under my breath. I assumed someone from the camera crew had forgotten something in the house. When I reached the door, I couldn't believe who stood there.

It was Jennifer.

She had been staking out the house with her dad, hiding in his Jeep and waiting for us to arrive. She just wanted to make sure we got home safely and didn't intend to come in. Once everyone else had left, however, Jen knew it would be impossible to resist seeing us. She was wearing a surgical mask to avoid exposure to any viruses while immuno-compromised, but above it, her eyes smiled enough to make all of us incredibly happy. Zoey spotted Jennifer and stood up, stopped crying at once, and then walked over to gently touch the glass that separated them.

Jen couldn't hug or kiss the kids, so we kept the door closed and talked through the glass. Will and Zoey were confused, but they kept their composure just like their mom. I can't say their dad fared as well. Tears streamed down my face. I was a bit of a wreck—both happy to see my wife and disappointed that I couldn't give her a hug. Yet as I watched her interactions with her kids, smiling and laughing, another emotion filled me.

How incredible is this woman standing beyond that glass?

This was a snapshot of spirit, a true image of someone being courageous. Jen was undergoing intensive treatment and fighting for her life, yet she was standing there trying to make *us* feel better. Her voice and demeanor were calm and upbeat. As always, Jen was trying to stay positive.

I don't think she had any idea what it meant to see her right then.

In that moment I saw just how she was going to fight the cancer: on her own terms, in her own way. Showing up at our doorway sick and surely exhausted, Jen wasn't going to let the mask she wore hide her grin. And she wasn't about to let this cancer destroy her spirit. I could see clearly what Jen believed.

Cancer is not going to win.

Witnessing this, I not only believed it, too, but I felt a surge of strength go through me. I wasn't on my own, and neither was Jen. We were going to meet this challenge head-on, together. And we would win.

It wouldn't be the first time we'd faced challenges.

- - - - - - - - -

Both for Jen and for me, the first forty years of life have been filled with challenges. We were both born with a rare form of dwarfism, called spondyloepiphyseal dysplasia (SED). SED is characterized by short stature and a range of medical complications that have to do with the skeletal system. It affects approximately 1 in 100,000 births and is the product of a random genetic mutation, unless one of your parents has SED. And while having a disability of this nature is difficult to manage, painful to live with, and usually requires many adaptations to function "normally," it is possible to lead a happy and prosperous life. We are two cases in point.

People ask us all the time how we both have such positive attitudes, despite all the challenges we've faced. These challenges could have led to emotional turmoil and negativity. We could have let our differences get the better of us, keeping us from being all we could be. So what happened? people ask us. How did we end up being so optimistic?

That is what this book is about. What has touched us and forged our resilience. And more importantly, what we now turn to time and time again as new challenges continue to arise.

Unfortunately, there is no magic pill to take. But we have come up with something of a philosophy to live by, a way of approaching life. In this book, we would like to introduce to you our mantra: Think Big.

From everyday challenges to life-changing decisions, Thinking Big has gotten us through a lot. We think of each letter in those words as a sort of "tool" to our toolbox.

THINK BIG

T is for try: You never know what you can accomplish in life unless you first try.

H is for hope: Nothing can be accomplished without the hope of accomplishment.

I is for initiate: What first step can you take today toward the goal you want to achieve?

N is for no: Never listen to the no's.

K is for know: Know your limitations.

B is for believe: Never stop believing.

I is for improve: Always continue to strive to improve, even if you achieve your goals in life.

G is for go for it: Identify one thing you are going to do and just go for it.

These are the words we live by. We try to explore every opportunity and complete every task using this approach. Remembering to Think Big helps us give an honest and complete effort to everything we do. When we Think Big, it becomes less important whether we succeed or fail, and more important how we approach any given situation. Think Big is a way of thinking that has radically changed our lives, and we hope that by sharing some of what we've learned, it will help you as well.

Jen and I believe that if you apply Think Big to your challenges, big and small, you'll find greater success. You'll also recognize greater satisfaction with your journey toward achievement and find joy in the things that matter most.

We have shared this Think Big idea in some of our talks, and we have found that people always respond well. Not everybody has spondyloepiphyseal dysplasia, but everybody has something difficult they are facing. Everybody has challenges every day that feel too big to endure. No matter what obstacles you face, we believe Think Big can help you approach them with optimism and courage. Our hope is that our words will help you feel like you, too, can face any challenge.

To illustrate the points we're making in this book, we're going to use examples from our lives. From childhood experiences to some of the most serious adult situations a human being can face, you will see how Think Big has helped us in nearly everything we do; and how it can help you to achieve your goals, too.

Laugh with us, cry with us, and Think Big with us.

CHAPTER ONE

TRY

"Just try to be the best you can be; never cease trying
to be the best you can be. That's in your power."

—John Wooden

PULL YOURSELF UP

Jen

The merry-go-round looked like a brightly lit castle with a parade of sparkling animals running around it. We had been exploring the grounds of the 1982 World's Fair in Knoxville, Tennessee, all day, but nothing captivated me like this particular ride. I spotted a massive white horse, looking gallant with its golden bridle and glittering saddle, and just knew I had to ride it.

There was just one little catch: the cast on my leg that weighed twenty pounds and went from my hip to my toes.

As an eight-year-old, I didn't see how I could even get up on

1

any of the horses on the carousel, much less hold on to it as it went round and round. But I desperately wanted to ride it. I don't think I'd ever wanted to climb on top of anything more in my life than this fixed creature on the merry-go-round.

"I never get to ride anything fun," I said in my best attempt at playing the sympathy card. Dad simply smiled, refusing to listen to any of my complaining.

"Why don't we just try it out?" he suggested.

Of course, it's natural for parents to encourage their child by helping to push them along and give them confidence. But both of us knew I wasn't an ordinary child. Typical children don't have ten surgeries by the time they reach eight years old. Many things looked different from my vantage point. Especially since I had to look up at the rest of the world most of the time. We never viewed my stature as a disability. Sometimes, however, as in moments like this, I had to carry a little extra baggage.

I was coming off my tenth surgery. When school had finished that May, I had been admitted to Johns Hopkins Hospital and went through a procedure called an osteotomy. Even though I was only eight, I knew the drill.

The surgery would attempt to correct the abnormal curvature of my left leg and normally took between four and six hours to perform. An incision was made on the outer side of my leg, and soft tissue and muscle were moved to the side to expose the bone. The surgeon would use a saw to cut the bone in half, remove a small angular piece of bone, and then rejoin the two halves. Normally, a plate and screws or large stainless-steel staples would fix the bone in place. At the end of the procedure, my leg was wrapped in a plaster cast to immobilize the limb for a period of up to three months while it healed.

Since I'd started visiting hospitals and having surgeries at the ripe old age of two, our family had the whole process down by this point. My mom would pack our suitcase and make the fifteen-hour trek to Baltimore. After arriving at the hospital, we would try to find the doctor's office. This wasn't as easy as it sounds. Hopkins was a huge place. They had used color-coding to help people find their way, but I'm pretty sure it was just more confusing. We would meet the doctor, review the plan of action, and then try to relax until the surgery the following day.

I would be one of the fortunate souls to have Dr. Steven Kopits as my surgeon. He would go on to become my lifelong orthopedist and friend. Of course, as a child, all I knew was that surgery always ended up putting my life on pause. That's why our visits to the hospital were always planned out well in advance.

Bones heal over time, not overnight. And so my mom and dad often thought it best to have my surgeries in the summer whenever possible in order to avoid any negative impact to my scholastic progress. At the time I wondered why I wasn't free to roam the beach, playing with friends and collecting seashells in the sand during the summers. Of course, looking back now, I see my parents were definitely looking out for my best interests.

At the time, though, I still longed to simply be like any other kid. To be able to sprint into the warm waters of the ocean or to spring up onto an elegantly decorated horse ready to begin its steady march on the merry-go-round. And when I couldn't, it made me ask the question:

Why can't I just do what everyone else does?

This was the case at that World's Fair in 1982. I stood staring at the gleaming carousel in front of me, knowing I couldn't spring up onto anything. I would have to watch the ride, just like I had been doing all day.

"Come on, let's give it a try," my father said.

My parents always tried to encourage me to try different things, even when it seemed like the road ahead was impossible. Their encouragement gave me the courage to try new things. Sports, for instance. I tried playing baseball and soccer, and I discovered I was terrible at both. But I also began to play the piano and ended up loving it. Without my parents' encouragement, I know I would have missed out on a lot of things. This was just one of the many times I needed to be pushed a bit.

My parents had known that visiting the World's Fair that summer would be a once-in-a-lifetime opportunity, something this scholastic overachiever would appreciate, even if I was only eight. As Mom pushed my brother, David, in a stroller, I sat on a rented wheelchair, since I had the cast and would have been too cumbersome to carry around for too long.

We had walked around the fairgrounds, taking in the attractions gathered around a man-made lake. One of them had been a giant gold sunsphere tower. Some of the other highlights of the fair included new inventions, such as Cherry Coke and the touchscreen display. Of course, the most popular items at the fair were the arcade games such as *Pac-Man* and *Donkey Kong*, and the brand-new *Rubik's Cube*. We had an Atari at our house, but I was more into schoolwork than video games, and I was more interested in the amusement park rides.

Eventually we wound up in front of that glorious merry-go-round. All I could see was how impossible it would be for me, yet my dad assured me I could do it.

"How do you know if you can't do it unless you try?" he said, sizing up the ride. "We can do this. We just need to do it a little creatively."

He wasn't going to force me to do anything. Hearing his encouragement, however, was enough for me. I would go ahead and try to ride it. As we joined the line, my fears began to heighten, yet I knew my dad was at my side and wouldn't let anything happen. I continued to look for the pretty white-and-gold horse as it circled by me.

Once it was our turn to go on the ride, my dad lifted me out of the wheelchair and carried me onto the merry-go-round. We found my perfect horse and he sat me down in the saddle to assess the situation.

"You're going to need something to secure your leg," he told me.

"I don't want to get off," I said.

Dad has always been a quick thinker, and this time he didn't disappoint. He took off his belt and wrapped it around my leg, and then around the pole in front of the horse's saddle. With my leg suspended on the side of the horse, my dad stepped back and gave me a chance to go for a ride. Of course, he wasn't too far away in case something went wrong. The carousel began to move and so did my horse. I held on to the pole and turned around to see my father standing there with a grin on his face.

Yes, it was just a simple ride at an amusement park. But for me, it stood for something far greater than that. It was another time my parents urged me to go ahead and give something a shot. To give it a try even if it seemed too difficult and scary. They could have understood my reluctance and held me back, or they could have stood there holding both of my arms. Yet they said it was possible, and then they gave me the courage to go ahead and try it out.

I would eventually have to get off that ride and climb back in that wheelchair, yet the encouragement my parents gave me that day still stands out to me as one time they helped me understand that I could give anything a shot, no matter how daunting it appeared to be.

GET BACK UP AFTER YOU FALL DOWN

Bill

But it's not enough to just try something out for the first time. Sometimes—many times, in fact—you have to be tenacious. You have to decide that you're really going to do this thing and go for it, regardless of the outcome. You have to tell yourself that no matter what happens today, there will be a tomorrow and you will try even harder. This can apply to a forty-year-old in his career, or it can apply to a five-year-old learning how to ride a bike.

6

Let me tell you about that first bike of mine.

On my fifth Christmas, I got my first set of wheels. She was metallic blue with spoke rims and white tires. She was gorgeous, and it was truly love at first sight for me. It was a unique little bicycle, to boot. It had a very comfortable tan leather seat, a single hand brake for the front wheel, reflectors galore, and it even came with an air pump for the impromptu roadside repair. And best of all, in the middle of the frame was a large white wing nut that, when removed, would allow the bicycle to fold completely in half for easy storage and transport.

The bike cost over $100, which was a lot of money to spend on a kid's bicycle back then. But it was worth every penny in my opinion.

She was custom made, just for me. A one-off that my grandfather (on my mom's side) and my father had had made for me. It was no small task, getting a bike for a kid that stood about twenty-eight inches tall with an eight-and-a-half-inch inseam. Toys R Us didn't stock them, nor did any of the bike shops close to my house, and anything anywhere close to my size was for babies anyway. And for a kid who stood just less than three feet tall, I had the mouth of someone three times my size. My parents knew a "baby bike" wouldn't do. I needed something similar (or better) than what everyone else was riding. It took them a long time to find one, but they would have one made in Italy and shipped to New York City the summer of '78. I would discover it months later sitting beside the Christmas tree.

That morning, I ran down the stairs as quickly as my little feet could carry me. I peered around the corner at the tree. My eyes grew huge as the package too big to fit under the tree came into view. The wrapping paper was draped over it in such a way that I couldn't quite tell what it was. Of course, back in the old days, we had rules about opening gifts before our parents woke up. It was a big no-no, so of course I immediately ran back upstairs and woke my parents. They slowly stumbled down the stairs, wrangled my little two-year-old brother Tom, and sat on the good couch in the living room next to the tree. Permission granted, I dove into the paper. I clawed and tore like some sort of monster or large house cat, and the gift began to appear.

Santa had done it again. I couldn't wait to ride my two-wheeler down the block. Thankfully, this two-wheeler had training wheels so I could learn how to balance on this beast before cruising into the sunset. Of course, winters in New York were rather unforgiving. Snow and ice were piled up along the sidewalks. I imagined zooming up and down the street, showing everyone on the block how fast I could go. But as soon as I led my bike out to the garage to try it out, I saw that icy sidewalks and puddles of unforgiving slush meant that my days of practicing would have to wait until spring.

When springtime eventually came, Dad helped me to the edge of the driveway. This would be my launch pad, and where I would often crash in a feeble, sometimes miraculous, and always breathtaking (for Mom) attempt to arrive home. He held the bike steady while I climbed onto the crossbar and finally lowered my butt onto the seat. Grasping the little white handlebar grips as tight as could be, Dad instructed me to take my feet off the crossbar.

"Okay, now put your feet on the pedals," Dad said.

I tried, and realized I couldn't reach them.

When I had done this sitting in the living room, I could reach both pedals, since the crank had been parallel to the floor. But in the real world, your foot needs to be on the pedal the whole time to make revolutions, and my legs fell a bit short. As luck would have it, even this custom-made bicycle was too big for me.

Day one on my bike was a failure.

A complete failure.

With a pouting face and a head hung low, I climbed down from my bicycle and went back into the house.

Sure, I could have given up, but come on. I just had to ride that bike. Nothing was going to stop me from doing it. The following weekend, Dad rolled the bike out into the driveway. This time around, there was a new addition to my new bicycle—pedal extensions. These were the first of what would be a lifelong companion for me in any vehicle I would drive. These extensions weren't much more than a piece of wood strapped to each side of the pedal, held together by a rather large rubber band.

"Let's try this again," Dad said as I climbed onto the bicycle seat again. I placed my feet on each of the pedals, and Dad continued to firmly hold the bicycle in place. I began to start pedaling and couldn't believe when the wheels began to turn. My feet actually stayed on the pedals. I'd finally done it.

For a moment, I thought I had overcome the hardest part. How naïve a five-year-old can be.

For a few weeks we'd repeat the same routine of Dad holding

the bicycle upright while I pedaled along. Sometimes Dad would get distracted, but the training wheels were there to back both of us up. We'd go up and down the sidewalk and eventually head back up the driveway with my dad pushing me faster by gripping the handlebars. But both of us eventually grew bored with this routine. I wanted to be able to ride a two-wheeler, and my dad wanted to go back inside.

It turns out that learning to ride a bike for the first time is quite a lot harder than it looks. I was pedaling on my own, but I hadn't figured out how to balance the bicycle. The training wheels were great at keeping me from landing on my face, but they weren't instilling any confidence in my ability to ride without them. So my father and I continued to practice with the training wheels on, seemingly with no end in sight. There was no sign of when they would be replaced by balance and skill.

Summer arrived, and school was out. Most of my friends were also still learning how to ride bicycles. But the friend closest to me, geographically and socially, was my best friend and neighbor, Andria. She was ten months older than I was (and still is today). That meant she was a grade above me, and better than me in nearly everything we did together. But Andria was definitely one of my very best friends and still is to this day.

Andria lived two houses down from me and had an older brother, Chris. She had long brown hair, brown eyes, and a medium complexion. She was a cutie for sure. But because she was also the younger sibling, and most of her friends were boys, she tended to be more of a tomboy than a girly girl. That was all right by me. We used to get into trouble together, raid each other's fridges together. In fact, if we were not at school it was more than likely that we were together.

One of the things she and I had discussed at length was our dream of freedom. That is, freedom to ride our bicycles around the neighborhood without our parents and away from our siblings. But this dream would only be recognized on two wheels, and neither of us had mastered that skill as yet. But we knew the summer was long, and we were both determined to learn how to ride.

One day in July, either due to the heat, humidity, or plain frustration, my dad did the unthinkable. We walked to the curb as we had done every weekend for the past few months, but this time my dad had a ratchet in his hand. It wasn't the size ratchet you needed for tightening brakes or adjusting the seat. This was a bigger ratchet. This was a ratchet used to take off training wheels.

Sometimes mother birds push their young out of the nest as encouragement to fly. As they hurl toward the ground, many of them spread their wings and soar up into the clouds. A few simply crash. Let's just say I was one of the latter.

My parents were always very encouraging. They knew it was important for me to try to do new things and to occasionally fail. Their attitude on raising a child with a disability was that my disability would curtail my activity only to the degree they protected me from experiencing success and failure when trying to do something new. So that meant sometimes they let me crash.

My dad removed the pedals, stood the bike up, and held it for me as I climbed on. The sensation of sitting on a two-wheeler was completely new and awkward. I no longer had the stability and confidence of the training wheels to prevent me from falling. Dad held the handlebar steady and allowed me some time to acclimate to this new reality. I was so nervous that my first day without training wheels ended before it began. After just a minute or two of sitting on the bike I loved so much, I climbed down, sulking, and returned to the house.

The toughest part about trying was learning to appreciate failure and understanding how to use it as encouragement to try again.

In the few weeks that followed, I showed little sign of improvement. I would climb on the bicycle, Dad would firmly hold the bike in place, and I would slowly pedal down the sidewalk, constantly reminding him not to let go.

In August, we finally had a breakthrough, but I didn't know it. I did the same as before. I climbed on the bike, sat down, and began pedaling with Dad in tow. Or so I thought. By the midway point, my dad shouted to me from what sounded like a mile away.

"You're doing it," he called out.

At which point I promptly crashed into a bush. There were no cuts, no bruises—it should have been a successful first two-wheeled experience. However, I didn't see it that way. Because I hadn't given the directive that it was okay to let go, I got angry with Dad and stormed back into the house. I left the bicycle on the lawn near the "crash site" and went up to my room.

The way I saw it that day, my dad letting go of the seat and letting me ride until I crashed was a betrayal of trust. I could not believe he would let me go.

What I could not appreciate at the time was that the risk my father took in letting go of the seat was necessary. Moreover, as a dad to two children just about to learn how to ride bicycles themselves, I am absolutely sure it was more painful for him to let go than it was for me to crash into the bush.

The next weekend, I skipped our weekend ride. For a five-year-old, I was pretty good at making a statement. Dad took notice, but didn't push me. Moreover, football season had begun once more, and he wasn't about to miss a chance to see an entire game, so I don't think he was too heartbroken.

Several weeks passed without any more attempts at riding that bike. But then the day came when Andria knocked on my front door. She bounced around at my stoop with incredible enthusiasm. It was at that moment she announced that she had finally learned how to ride a bike without training wheels. She was proud to show off her newly learned feat and seemingly ride off into the sunset.

That's it.

Now I was on a mission. I stumbled through the dark garage, unlocked the door from the inside, and opened it up just enough for me and my bicycle to escape underneath it. I dragged Dad outside for one more attempt. Yet this time, I was the one who told him to let me go. I pedaled as fast as I could down the sidewalk. Dad let go of the seat and I continued on. The first big bump was coming up. My apprehension was tossed aside as I accelerated over the bump. Pushing each pedal toward the ground took all my might. I practically threw my body into each revolution. Much to his surprise, I didn't stop at the end of the sidewalk. Instead, I made a right turn at the neighbors' driveway and accelerated into the street. Now I had some momentum.

The wind against my face, my hands tightly grasping the handlebars, I glanced out of the corner of my eye, as if to give the nod to my dad to say "thanks" and "I am doing it" all at once. I kept pedaling all the way down to Andria's house. I rode up onto her driveway, ditched the bike on her lawn, and ran to the door. I knocked furiously on the screen door, and when she opened the door, I simply stated, "I can ride, too," and walked back to my bike.

Trying something can be scary, and it can also be hard work. You can try and fail and try and fail again. Failing in this case literally meant crashing (but thankfully not burning). Sure, you might walk away with some scrapes or a bruised ego. But unless you're naturally gifted, you'll have to practice over and over until you have the skills you need to do what you imagine.

The worst thing isn't going for something and making a fool of yourself. It's sitting on the sidelines safe and sound while you have to watch others soar on by. It's sitting and knowing that you didn't even take a chance; that you stopped bothering to try.

BE OPEN TO NEW IDEAS

Jen

There are many things Bill and I might have thought we'd be willing to try in our lives, but starting a reality show was certainly not one of them. In fact, even after being asked numerous times to do one, we turned down the opportunity. Sometimes the timing just has to be right in order to go ahead and give something a shot. This was exactly the case for *The Little Couple*.

In the fall of 2007, someone from *Good Morning America* called me to say they were interested in having me on an upcoming show they were going to do about Little People. They wanted to show the juxtaposition between the stereotypes that were out there and examples of women who had successful careers despite their diminutive statures. After contacting Little People of America, a support group for people who are short in stature, my name was mentioned, and suddenly I was given an invitation to be on television.

At the time, we were living in Port Jefferson Station, Long Island, and I was working in the NICU—the neonatal intensive care unit—at Stony Brook University Medical Center (now called Stony Brook University Hospital). I thought the interview would be a great opportunity to shed some light on skeletal dysplasia and educate some viewers about living a prosperous life as a Little Person. So the first thing the crew from ABC did was to come to the hospital in Long Island and shoot some B-roll of me working. Next they asked to do the interview with Bill and me at our home.

Bill had just come from a business trip, taking a red-eye flight home. And even though he was exhausted from the long trip, he was nice enough to clean up the house before I arrived home with the camera crew. He even bought some flowers for the room in which we would conduct the interview. Our interview would take place around the kitchen table. Since Bill and I both love our coffee—we normally have two cups in the morning—we naturally shared it with the reporter interviewing us. Bill poured us all cups, and then we sat for the next hour talking about people with disabilities.

The segment would air on November 30, 2007. After all the filming and discussion, the segment would only be a couple minutes long. The other woman being interviewed was in the entertainment industry so she shared her story, and then it focused on me talking about what it took to get through medical school and what it was like working in a hospital. They showed thirty seconds of me at the table in our house talking. The only glimpse of Bill that got shown was him serving us coffee. That still makes us laugh to this day.

When the segment was finished and the hosts of *Good Morning America* began to talk, they mentioned that the man serving the coffee just so happened to be my fiancé, and we were planning on getting married the following April. This would be the single piece of information that would work its way to a production company and would plant a seed of an idea.

A month later, we received a call from LMNO Productions, Inc. They were a leading producer of network and cable reality shows. The executive producer had seen my interview and was interested in following the preparation and events leading up to and including our wedding.

Bill and I talked about the idea for maybe a few seconds before deciding to pass. It wasn't out of fear, but more because of where we were both at with our careers. Sure, maybe we'd end up getting some money that would help pay for some of our wedding costs, but we didn't necessarily want to show our lives on television. We were concerned about how it might impact our jobs and our reputations. There wasn't much to talk about before saying no. So, after breaking the news to them that we had decided to say thanks but no thanks, they asked if we could stay in touch. Moreover, if they came up with a better idea, would we be willing to hear them out. We assumed that would be the last of it.

They were certainly interested, and for the next six months they would periodically call us. Even after we got married and I ended up pursuing a new job, the offer to do a reality show kept being tossed at us.

"We have a new idea," the producer told us. "We'd like to chronicle your lives, to show both your personal and professional lives. We'd film you at your work and then at home."

Once again, Bill and I told them no. We had already been in the "Try" mode, as I considered a new job opportunity in a very different setting. Moving to Texas would already change our lives in many ways, so adding a reality television show on top of this seemed out of the question.

I had grown up seeing the power of physicians and hospitals and medical staff, and how they helped people on a daily basis. This was why I went into medicine—I knew what this field was like since I'd grown up in it, and I wanted to build a career caring for others just like I'd been taken care of. What I didn't realize, though, was the power that existed to help people through the world of entertainment.

That changed when I was stopped at the supermarket by a young girl who walked right up to me as if she had known me her whole life.

"You're a Little Person, like *Little People, Big World*."

For a moment, I couldn't believe what she had just said. It was the first time I had been in public and heard a stranger use the term "Little Person."

She didn't use the M-word.

She was referring to another reality television show on TLC that had been out for more than a year called *Little People, Big World*. It featured two short-statured parents and their four children. This girl didn't seem apprehensive, and she wasn't making fun of me. Instead, she appeared delighted to see me, as if I was some type of celebrity. The show had taught this girl not only the right terminology, but also that it was no big deal to be a Little Person. This brief interaction suddenly opened up a world of possibilities.

She got it. And if someone this young got it, what about someone older? Could a reality show really help educate viewers about life as a Little Person?

After working so hard in school and with my medical training, I knew I couldn't do anything that would detract from my career or my reputation. But I suddenly saw the idea of a reality show in a whole new light. Maybe we could show a different angle to life as Little People.

Bill was on the same page immediately. He understood my newfound respect for what a show like *Little People, Big World* was doing. We took a look at the other reality shows out there, and most of them offered these unique stories in very specific environments, whether they were on a farm or in a family business. Most of the people shown were in very contained environments, while Bill and I were in busy jobs, living in a regular apartment in an urban environment. Our lives would truly represent two young professionals starting to build a life together. The only difference would be our short stature and the perception others had of us.

When we spoke again to the producer, we agreed to try it. They'd film a pilot. We knew the probability of the show being successful was very slim. All we wanted was to make sure we didn't make complete fools of ourselves.

Sometimes in the world of trying, it's not about mustering up the courage to go for it; it's about managing to find absolute certainty in the decision to move ahead. Sometimes you have to say no a few times before you know it's the right time to say yes. The little girl showed me a reason to give it a shot. So this Little Couple would try doing a reality show to see where it might take us. And the rest is hist— Well, more on that below.

CHANGE CAN BE GOOD

Bill

There's nothing more exciting on reality television than watching someone working for a consulting firm. Five conference calls and checking email and going through a contract—now that is absolutely riveting stuff.

I used to joke about this with our producers anytime they were looking for new angles and ideas of what to feature on our show. I was all for any new sort of ideas, but I also made it clear I had a full-time job I needed to attend to. For the longest time, our reality show never really covered what I did for a living. I'm sure there were probably people who watched our show and wondered what my career was.

"So what's this grifter doing with our sweet Dr. Arnold? When's he going to get a job and get a life?"

The truth was that I was running a successful consulting company with twenty employees. I was proud of what my partner and I had done with our company, but I also knew nobody wanted to watch me in action.

I had always been one of the hardest workers around. My lousy love life had probably helped this in immeasurable ways. Like on New Year's Eve before the world was supposed to end on January 1, 2000—also known as the dreaded Y2K. I was the only guy in the company who volunteered to stay and watch all the computers in our office as the clock struck midnight. So there I was, very single and very hardworking, watching the computers do nothing. Just me and my four-pack of Guinness (Draught cans, not the Extra Stout bottles), ready for the apocalypse.

I had started the consulting firm with my partner back in 2005, a year before I would officially meet and fall for Jen. Moving had never been factored into the equation when we first spoke about our business. Getting married and moving to Texas? That was something I couldn't have imagined, but that's exactly what happened in 2008. Still, we decided that I'd stick with my partner and see how things would work out long distance.

Things went fine for a while. That first year I commuted back and forth every week, first staying at my old house in Long Island until I sold it, then living in hotel rooms or staying with my mother. I would discover that with love, distance did make the heart grow fonder. As far as work was concerned, though, the distance simply made life more tedious.

Honestly, I really just wanted someplace to hang my hat locally.

For two and a half years I did my best to make it work, but I knew that I needed to make a change. So in 2011 I sold the equity I had in the partnership and decided to try something completely new. I knew I didn't want to replicate what I'd been doing in New York. I've realized something about myself over the years—I'm more of a creator than a manager. I love to build something and then hand it over to someone to run with. That's why as I began to look for a new venture, I knew I didn't want to get into sales or operational management. I also knew I didn't want to go back into the workforce and work for someone else. I had had a taste of being an entrepreneur and didn't want that to end.

So what could I do down here in Houston?

An idea kept coming to me in different forms. First off, I began to wonder what it would be like to go into retail. To have an actual brick-and-mortar business. To work with consumers one-on-one. I hadn't ever been on this side of the fence in the business world, so the idea felt exciting and fresh. It would be a new and different experience.

If there was ever a time to go ahead and try something out like this, it was now. Jen supported the idea.

"I'll support you as you build a new business," she told me.

Jen was working. I had sold my house in New York and had money in the bank. And we were also generating some income from our show. I figured I might enjoy working retail. Plus, I would be able to include it from time to time on the show. We didn't have any illusions that our business would grow exponentially because of occasionally being featured on the show, but we figured, why not try the retail world out?

And a wild idea came to mind.

How about opening a pet business?

It wasn't such a crazy thought, to be honest. I had grown up around cats and dogs. I'd probably owned around ten cats and dogs in my life. The following is a (likely incomplete) list of the pets we had over the years:

Lassie—This was a calico cat that ended up having eight kittens. We gave them to all of our relatives and friends.

Coffee—An adopted dog from a friend. He was a mix that looked like a miniature golden retriever.

Rascal—A schnauzer that loved to have someone scratch his back. He also was notorious for tunneling under our fence and running away. Once he ran eight miles away to another town. Thankfully, his tag was still on and he was reunited with us after just a few days of gallivanting around.

There was another dog my parents had when I was just one year old. It was a big dog and quite nutty. I guess after my parents brought me home, it put this dog over the edge because one day it literally jumped through an open window and ran away. For the sake of this story, let's call him Dutch.

Midnight and Teddy Bear—Midnight was a Yorkie Maltese and the other a poodle Maltese. They were related by their Maltese ancestor, so we referred to them as cousins. They looked very different—one was a teddy bear and the other black and brown and funky-looking. We had them for a long time. Midnight used to sleep on me when I was in a body cast. I'd never notice until I woke up the following morning. Teddy's white face would become red since she had an affinity for pizza and pasta.

Belle—We got Belle from a local rescue just before Jen and I got married. We had put our name on the list at the local shelter in Port Jefferson, looking for a dog that would not grow to be a monster. We received a call and I went to pick up Belle the evening before I left for Florida to catch up with Jen and her family. What I didn't know was that Belle, while cute and playful, was destined to grow . . . a lot. So much so that when I went for surgery to have my hips replaced, Jen couldn't walk Belle, as she was just too darn strong. So, as we migrated to Texas, Belle stayed behind with her short-term dog sitter, soon to be long-term owner, my mom. Belle still resides at my mom's house with her and Chuck. Belle has an awesome home there.

I also had countless gerbils, newts, fish, and a turtle. My brother Tom had a few birds (Tweety I, II, and III).

Having pets wasn't just something I loved growing up—it was still a very important part of my life. Jen and I loved our two dogs—Rocky and Maggie—and truly considered them our first two children. We had been customers shopping for our pets for quite some time. We knew that world well.

I realized something about a pet shop. Nobody ever entered a pet store in a bad mood. You could be having the worst day in the world, then go to pick up some dog food and be reminded of your loving animal waiting for you at home. I liked the idea of building a business around consumers who were happy at the very thought of purchasing something in our store. Why not surround myself with customers who were animal-lovers like Jen and me?

Of course, I didn't go into this just on a whim. I did a lot of research and even went to a couple of trade shows to take a look around. I spoke to vendors and retailers. I would discover that a pet shop is really quite recession resistant. People were always going to own pets and they always had to feed them and take care of them.

So February 3, 2012, Rocky & Maggie's Pet Shop opened at 2535 Times in Rice Village, a shopping district in Houston. Our shop would feature food, treats, beds, leashes, carriers, clothing, grooming services, and other dog and cat paraphernalia. And almost four years later, the store has grown and we're continuing to try out lots of fun and different things with it.

Some decisions in life can be simple and others can be life-and-death. Then there are those that remain somewhere in the middle, moments and opportunities where a door might close and a window might open. Many times we just stand and look out the window studying the scene outside.

But occasionally, you need to go ahead and be like Dutch, the first pet I ever knew. You have to just take a leap and go for it, to try something new. And, well, in that crazy dog's case, to start a whole new life, whatever it might be.

THERE'S NO HARM IN TRYING

Jen

Before even starting a family, Bill and I became aware of a girl's sad situation through the Little People of America organization. A very cute girl from Russia had been adopted by a family in the U.S., but the family hadn't known this girl was a Little Person. After they realized it, they decided not to adopt her. So there she was, the precious young girl now living in the States in need of a family to care for her. LPA was trying to help her find a home.

Bill and I had followed the LPA message boards and continued to follow her story. What could we do, and how could we help? The whole situation felt so tragic, and we couldn't believe how awful she must have felt and how imperative it was that she found a family to love and care for her.

That's when we first began to wonder: *What if we adopted?* It was just an idea. One that really came out of nowhere.

There was never that one moment when I woke up with a grand epiphany that this was how we would start a family. It was always something I thought about, and I wondered whether it would happen. Bill and I talked a lot about the idea since we both wanted children. There were obviously many questions that came to mind, though. Everybody has questions about timing and finances and careers and all of that when factoring in becoming parents. But as a Little Person, there were a lot more questions I had to consider.

The questions brought quite a bit of uncertainty. I wasn't doubtful that I could realistically get pregnant, but to carry a biological child could be risky. Even as we dated, Bill and I discussed the idea of whether I could have a child. There were different ways to have children, though. What about adoption?

A part of me had always wanted to adopt a Little Person. Even before I met Bill, while I wasn't sure about having a child myself, I had always told myself that one day I'd adopt a Little Person. So when those dark eyes and round cheeks were brought to our attention, we suddenly asked whether that dream could become a reality.

I knew someone at LPA involved with the adoption process, so I emailed her to ask some questions. I asked Colleen if there was any way we could be considered for the girl's parents. Colleen told us that there was actually a waiting list, and if we were serious about adopting, we would need to fill out a lot of paperwork first. There would be home studies and approvals needed before we could be considered a proper home. Needless to say, we had little idea of what was involved, but we would soon learn.

"If you guys are serious, I can put your names on the list," she told us.

So even before we married, Bill and I put our names on it. Why not? It seemed scary, almost overwhelming, but we figured, what harm could it do to simply give them our names? We didn't really think about it for a long time. There was nothing wrong with trying to pursue that path if it indeed opened up.

Neither of us had any idea what our path toward parenthood would look like. Nobody does. We were hopeful and simply exploring options and willing to give something a try.

We didn't end up adopting that little girl from Russia. At that point we hadn't even started any of the necessary steps to become approved for adoption. She deserved to find a loving home immediately, and thankfully, she found one with a family in the LPA community. So we continued down our path and tried to have a baby using a surrogate. But because we put our names on the list, it was only a matter of time before our names reached the top. Looking back, if we hadn't tried to open our home for that girl, we may never have pursued adoption as the way we would create a family. We may never have realized the joy we would get from a boy named Will from China and a girl named Zoey from India. I can't imagine what our lives would have been like without them. And we would never have gotten them if we hadn't been willing to try something that at the time seemed crazy.

Sometimes you start down one path and find yourself in a completely different place from where you started. Usually, you learn that this was the path you were always intended to travel down. But starting the journey, trying to take that very first step, is often the most important part.

SET YOURSELF FREE

Bill and Jen

Life is all about trying. It's easy to wake up wanting something, wondering if it will happen. But it takes a lot of courage to go ahead and actually try to make it happen. It's safe to settle for less by sitting on the sideline. But stepping up to achieve your goal—that's worth any amount of risk in our opinions.

Yes, you might fall off your horse. *Literally.* You might even fall off the entire merry-go-round.

Sure, you will probably crash your bike while learning to ride on two wheels.

Maybe the chances are high you'll end up looking silly sometimes if you say yes to a reality television show.

There's always the possibility your new store—no matter how creative and clever a concept it happens to be—will fail.

And yes, you might end up hoping and planning and praying for a family, but it might not happen.

The worst might indeed happen. But it probably won't. Usually, it will be just the opposite. More often than not, you'll feel the thrill of a ride for the first time in your life, and feel safe knowing that someone has your back. You'll end up racing for the first time in your life and discover that you love speeding. You'll step onto that platform and share a little more of your life in a unique way in order to help others lean in and learn. You'll plunge into a new venture and discover new challenges and creations you never imagined.

You might just even discover the world is no longer just about you trying out new things. You might discover that it's about helping two other precious souls learn to try new things for themselves.

Is there something you've been thinking about, something you want to do or some job you want to pursue or some dream you've always thought you might chase someday? What's holding you back from trying today?

Trying anything new can be scary. But when you stop listening to those worries, about the labels you've imposed on yourself, you'll realize that YOU have the power to take that scary first step. You might have to do it differently, but you can do it.

And just like on that first merry-go-round or that first bike ride, you'll often discover that once you get going, nothing can stop you.

TRY THIS OUT

1. Make a little list of big dreams. Think about things you had always wanted to achieve but maybe were afraid to. Write them in an email to yourself or on a note in your phone or simply on a sheet of paper.

2. Write one corresponding thing you can do to try to help make that dream happen.

3. Set a crazy deadline for your dreams to happen. Write down a very specific date to shoot for.

4. Keep this list on hand so you can see it daily. Keep it there to remind yourself to keep trying.

CHAPTER TWO

HOPE

"When I was young, my ambition was to be one of the
people who made a difference in this world. My hope is to
leave the world a little better for having been there."

—Jim Henson

CELEBRATE THOSE WHO BRING IT

Jen

I watched the door from my hospital bed, fighting to keep my eyes open, trying not to get too comfortable. The word "comfort" doesn't usually apply when you've just had your bones broken, realigned, and stitched up again, but by the time you're fourteen years old you've grown used to having osteotomies. And since it was late—almost eleven at night—the bed did feel more relaxing than it usually did during the day, and it was causing me to get drowsy. Well, the bed and the medication being administered to me intravenously. I was just hoping to see the doctor one more time before drifting off to discover what dreams awaited me.

Thankfully, on this particular night, it wasn't too long before my own personal Dr. McDreamy tapped on the door and entered the room. No, I wasn't dreaming. And no, his name wasn't Derek Shepherd from my favorite television show, *Grey's Anatomy*. This tall, dark, and handsome doctor happened to be Dr. Steven Kopits.

If there's someone who I truly believe should be named a saint, it's this man. The hope he brought to me on this late night when I was recovering from an intense surgery was the same sort of light he brought to hundreds of other Little People just like me on a daily basis.

"Hello, darling Jennifer. How are you feeling tonight?"

Dr. Kopits had a thick Hungarian accent, which made him sound both European and mysterious. He stood about six-foot-two-inches tall and spoke multiple languages effortlessly. He had been born in Budapest, Hungary, where his father and grandfather had been orthopedic surgeons. His grandfather founded Hungary's orthopedic society. This man would be filling very big shoes, but would eventually end up outgrowing them.

"I'm feeling okay," I said.

Even if I didn't feel okay I probably would have said this.

"At least you're not in a spica cast," Dr. Kopits said.

Whenever he operated on my hips, I would end up wearing

a full-body cast, known as a spica cast. This was one of the cases where he had only (only!) operated on my knee, and I was allowed to wear just a leg cast.

"Where's your mother?" he asked, looking around the room.

After each surgery, Mom would stay with me in the hospital room, sleeping on a cot at night. If my dad came he usually stayed at a hotel nearby.

"I think she's talking to some of the nurses down the hallway."

"Donna said she went over the care plan with you earlier," he said.

I told him she had. Donna was my primary nurse and could have almost been considered my own personal nurse because of all the time she spent with me. I've always said that Donna was my second mother. After each surgery Dr. Kopits would go over my postop and recovery regimen with Donna. The care plan covered everything, from what sort of medication I'd be on and what meals I would eat and what my morning baths would look like. Donna always had it covered.

There was a comfort in Dr. Kopits's voice and in his large presence. I'd grown up hearing and seeing him, ever since he first operated on me when I was two years old. That first surgery had been a cervical spine fusion, which Dr. Kopits and his colleague performed on me to help prevent spinal instability from rendering me paralyzed. The colleague who worked with him just so happened to be Dr. Ben Carson. That's right, that Ben Carson, MD—the presidential candidate and former neurosurgeon.

Dr. Kopits had moved from Hungary to Argentina just after

World War II. He studied in Buenos Aires and, ultimately, immi-
grated to the United States. He was the chief of pediatric orthope-
dics at Johns Hopkins Hospital in Baltimore in the 1960s and into
the 1970s. It was during that time, as he was ascending through the
ranks, that he became enamored of a particular group of patients.
He had previously treated a number of patients with skeletal dysplasias. And as he was exposed to the particulars each case presented,
he became more and more intrigued about this underserved community.

Dr. Kopits wound up dedicating his professional life to the
treatment and care of people with skeletal dysplasias. He would
often show up at the hospital before dawn. He'd get ready for surgery at six a.m., be in the operating room by seven thirty, and
wouldn't emerge from surgery until that evening. On his busier
days, he would do preoperative and/or follow-up visits from morning until evening. His patients, like me and Bill, would regularly
travel hundreds or thousands of miles and wait hours upon hours
just for a checkup. If you just had surgery and were still "living"
on the floor, you would commonly see Dr. Kopits at the end of his
workday. He would emerge from surgery, his office, or physical therapy and make his postoperative rounds on the floor. Oftentimes,
this meant you would see the doctor after ten p.m. and as late as
two a.m.

Just like this night.

Whenever he looked at you, his eyes conveyed a deep level of
sincerity. For patients, this helped calm the nerves. For the moms—
well, those eyes told a whole different story.

My mom, Judy, like all of the other moms, admired Dr. Kopits for all that he did for their children. Some moms more than admired him; they were enamored of him. And who wouldn't be? You could always tell when Dr. Kopits was arriving on the floor. Many of the moms, most wearing nightgowns or negligees with robes, would start scurrying about. I never really understood why everyone would fix their hair before they went to bed and keep their makeup on so late until I also became one of his groupies. If I could have fixed my hair and makeup, I would have done so, too.

The doctor never seemed too busy to make time to connect. The time spent with him never felt rushed and he never appeared distracted. Dr. Kopits was always present with you and he always gave hope regardless of what the situation or the outlook appeared to be.

Sometimes it wasn't what he said but how he said it. It was knowing that someone like Dr. Kopits was on my side, looking out for my best interests, and giving his whole life for people like me.

"I hope you're able to sleep well," Dr. Kopits said to me that night before he left. "I'll see you early tomorrow morning."

I wished him a good night, knowing he had already made mine that way.

I think part of why all of us love Dr. McDrea— I mean Dr. Kopits so much is that he gave us hope. He gave us hope that our stature didn't have to define us. He gave us hope that we could have normal lives, unlike so many previous generations of Little People before us.

The hope Dr. Kopits gave was stitched deep inside of me, and it eventually prompted me to try and follow in his footsteps. Some might have called that foolish, but not Dr. Kopits. He was the first one to give me the courage to apply to medical school. He knew I could follow in his footsteps, dedicating my life to helping others.

These bearers of hope in your life are rare, but their influence can be miraculous. When you do find them, never let go of them, and learn everything you can from them. Then carry that same light inside of you for others to see. The whole world can use a little more hope.

FIND HOPE IN ANYTHING

Jen

There are moments in your life when you have to cling to whatever hope you can find.

When I was two years old, there was a period of time when I really did resemble an angel with a halo. The halo wasn't over my head, however, but around it. The ring was made of metal and was part of a brace I was wearing after my cervical spine fusion, which had been performed by Dr. Kopits and Dr. Carson. The halo was attached to my head and pins held it in place, and it was kept from moving by metal bars connected to a vest I wore. The halo kept my head and neck still while allowing me to move around instead of being confined to a bed after recovering from surgery.

One particularly scary day, my head and neck were suddenly not so still, sending my parents into a panic.

As I said, I was two. Parents don't need to know anything more than that. There is a reason this age is often referred to as terrible. Children can walk, are trying to assert their independence, and develop personalities. By now they're often curious and strong-willed. In other words, they can make trouble and be stubborn. So imagine a two-year-old having to wear a halo. The only sort of angel you're going to find in this situation is the fallen sort.

On this day I had been crying so hard I pushed the metal pins screwed into my skull out of the halo ring. Suddenly my head and neck were loose. My dad ended up holding my head in place and forcing me not to move while he called my mom frantically at her work. Soon I'd be rushed out of the house into an ambulance headed back to the hospital to get my loose screws back in place.

I've often shared this story before, but this time I want to focus on a piece you haven't heard. While I was riding in the ambulance, my father was by my side trying to keep me calm. Trying to keep a scared and upset two-year-old calm isn't such an easy task. He had to think fast on his feet. But he held hope in his hand, in the form of a small stuffed lion.

My "Flying Lion."

And as the stuffed animal seemed to float above me and keep my attention, I heard my dad start to sing.

"The flying lion stops the crying."

Perhaps there's a reason why C. S. Lewis chose as the primary hero in his Narnia Chronicles a great lion, Aslan. There's just something about the king of the jungle. We're all enamored by this majestic animal, so children naturally love him.

My father probably realized this as well. The Flying Lion was accompanying me and protecting me and taking care of me. I suddenly knew that I was going to be okay. I saw the lion above my head as I felt the motion of the ambulance racing down the street. I heard the soothing song my dad was singing.

I looked up and knew I'd be okay. Someone was watching over me.

I would end up holding on to my Flying Lion and having him accompany me for the many upcoming surgeries I would have.

Obviously I didn't understand this at the time, but that lion represented hope to me. Through all those surgeries that stuffed lion represented the possibility that I would get through this one, too, as long as the Flying Lion was by my side.

I've come to realize that you need hope in your life, especially when things get tough. Even if your hope is unrealistic, it can also be very valuable. Having my Flying Lion with me gave me some comfort, and he was a reminder that my parents would always be there for me—sometimes in person and other times in spirit.

Flying Lion was there with me as I grew, and he gave me hope. There was also something else that gave me hope.

I was only ten years old when I had this crazy thought. This was about the time all the girls around me started talking about boys. I realized that I probably wasn't going to be finding a boyfriend anytime soon, and I was frustrated. I had always had friends and felt like I was a social person, but I suddenly felt the chasm of difference between me and the rest of the kids around me. I was a Little Person, and this was my life whether I liked it or not.

But what if . . .

A hope suddenly filled me.

Some kids have invisible friends. For me it was an invisible desire. Something that filled me with a sense of wonder and optimism.

Maybe I'm not really a Little Person after all. Maybe one day I'm going to wake up and discover that I'm just like everybody else.

I actually imagined that perhaps my mother had done something to my vision to have me look at the world differently. Or that one day my mom would tell me to take out the contact lenses she put in my eyes and I would see the world as a tall person. Moreover, that she would come to me and tell me she had wanted to give me a lesson about looking at the world from a different perspective.

I wasn't crazy, and I wasn't simply daydreaming. I was doing something—whatever it took—to inspire any kind of semblance of hope. At this young of an age, I was growing up like any other girl yet had a whole host of other realities forced upon me. So imagining the impossible—that one day I'd be tall—was a crazy hope.

What sort of kid would imagine something like this?

A kid trying to figure out her life and trying to find something—anything—to keep her spirits up.

Of course it was unrealistic and I am glad it never became a reality. But it was what I needed, just as I needed a Flying Lion when I was two. These things gave me hope, and that hope gave me the ability to face the hard reality of my life. As a child, choosing to have hope is a blessed thing. And the truth is, it is a choice. I didn't get to choose how tall I was, but I could choose to be optimistic and to find hope in something.

The idea that I'd someday wake up no longer little left me soon enough, though my stuffed lion never did. And hope has only continued to blossom in my life.

EMBRACE THE MOMENT

Bill

"I'm pregnant."

If I hadn't seen the positive results of the pregnancy test in Jen's hand, I don't think I would have believed what she was saying. She wasn't making a grand announcement—she was saying it in complete and utter disbelief.

"Well, I guess that was some family vacation," I said, as we both laughed at the insanity of the moment.

Only a month before we had taken Will down to Cape San Blas in Florida for our last outing as a family of three. We were going to be leaving for India to adopt Zoey in a few months and we had this premonition that going to the beach with one child would be far easier than heading there with two. Especially since Will was basically an old man in a kid's body who loved to watch the TV and stare out at the waves and sit on the sand content in all aspects of his life.

While in Florida, Jen and I had some much-needed rest and relaxation. A week on the beach was just what the doctor ordered. We played in the sand, we frolicked in the waves, we ate well; we got to enjoy being a family. We had fun.

Apparently too much fun.

Now, only weeks after the trip, Jen was pregnant. After going through two years of fertility treatments and surrogacy followed by miscarriages, this was unexpected, to say the least. We weren't trying and both thought there was no way it could happen. But *whamo* . . . it happened.

As we chuckled in disbelief with the sudden realization of what this meant, there was both joy and fear inside of us. All I could do was think the following:

God doesn't give you something you can't handle.

I had always believed this and had to remind myself once again.

If it's meant to happen it will happen.

After a long and heart-wrenching journey with surrogacy, Jen and I found ourselves suddenly in the center of a cyclone. We had just adopted one child and were about to head to India to adopt a second and *now we were expecting a third*?

As the realization kicked in, I have to admit something. I was freaking out a bit. The more I thought about going from having zero kids to three in less than a year, the more I realized that our hope had suddenly turned into something else.

I was going to go from having blond hair one day to being completely gray the next. Forget having a heart attack—I was going to be like the bad guy at the end of *Indiana Jones and the Last Crusade* when he drinks from the Holy Grail and it instantly ages him, turning him into a skeleton and then to dust. Some old knight in armor would be showing up at my front door and shaking his head.

"Bill chose . . . poorly," he would say.

Yet eventually my out of-body experience turned into more of a determined resolve.

It can be done. Why not us?

Hope had suddenly been dropped into our laps. Not once or twice but three times. Obviously there were the concerns that kept us from trying to have a baby the old-fashioned way. There were very real dangers because of Jen's stature, and we didn't know how she or the baby would fare. Those were very legitimate concerns. But right now we simply had to focus on what we knew. Will wasn't going anywhere, and we were planning our trip to India to meet Zoey and bring her back to our home. Beyond that, we would deal with the situation as it presented itself.

The thing some people don't realize about life but that Jen and I know very well is that there's no magic pill to help you handle things like this. You simply have to have an emotional resolve to face whatever comes. There are times you simply have to take a deep breath and ask yourself not if you can handle this but how you're going to make this work.

By the time we went to meet with Jen's ob/gyn, we were still skeptical, but also hopeful. There's a common saying: "Hope for the best and prepare for the worst." I've always liked the first part of that phrase. Yet as Jen and I entered the Texas Children's Hospital's Pavilion for Women, I knew I probably should fully embrace both parts of that expression.

We entered that exam room filled with hope and worry and curiosity, waiting to see what the ultrasound would reveal. Ultimately the truth came back as we had suspected. The ultrasound revealed that this was a nonviable pregnancy. We moved ahead as advised by Jen's ob/gyn and we scheduled an appointment to have a dilation and curettage (D&C) performed. We went to the hospital for the procedure and everything went as planned. The doctor told Jennifer they felt everything was removed and the tissue would be sent for pathological evaluation. They needed to evaluate for the possibility of a molar pregnancy. A week after the procedure, the results came back that the pregnancy had in fact been a complete molar pregnancy. Being the layman in the room, I didn't know what a molar pregnancy was, nor its potential significance. It's basically what happens when tissue that might otherwise develop into the placental tissue around a fetus becomes an abnormal growth in your uterus. Once the procedure was over, Jen and the obstetrician gave me the quick overview and explained how we would want to monitor Jen's beta HCG—the pregnancy hormone released into blood and urine, which incidentally is also the marker used in home pregnancy tests—to ensure it continued to drop over time.

We went for weekly blood draws, and everything seemed very normal. The hormone level was decreasing every week as expected. I felt relieved to know Jen didn't have to worry about the complications of being pregnant. Never would I have imagined that something worse was right around the corner. It turns out we wouldn't learn about it until we were on the opposite side of the world.

TAKE THE GOOD WITH THE BAD

Bill

There will be moments when the worst can and will happen. You can't spend your life worrying and waiting for them, but you can't crumble, either, when they suddenly appear. For me, the worst began the moment I woke up in another country and heard Jen's ominous words.

"Something's wrong."

Her voice sounded like it always did, but when I looked over at her standing across the hotel room, I could tell something was definitely wrong.

We were in Mumbai, India, to finally meet and bring home our daughter, Zoey Nidhi Klein, and had been there for two days when this new wrinkle developed in our plan.

"What happened?" I asked, assuming it had something to do with Will and Zoey or our nanny Kate or the film crew who had accompanied us on the trip.

"I woke up bleeding," she said.

I knew Jen wasn't talking about some kind of mysterious bug bite or injury she'd experienced. I instantly began to worry about the same thing that was troubling her.

This was one of those times I simply had to face head-on whatever would come our way. That would start by staying positive. We suspected the bleeding might have had something to do with the pregnancy surprise she'd had before we left, though the doctors had told us everything looked fine and her beta HCG levels had been going down. I knew I had to be strong for Jen and stay optimistic and remember that we were there for Zoey and that was what mattered.

Thankfully, we had already accomplished what we needed to in Mumbai to get our daughter. We went to Zoey's orphanage in a small bus, big enough for a camera crew, small enough to navigate the narrow streets in the city's center. I was struck by the parts of Mumbai we traveled through. To say the areas we traversed were destitute would be an understatement. I had seen shanties in movies and documentaries on television. But being up close and personal was a visceral experience. It was odd to depart from a hotel compound where the linens were changed nightly, where there was butler service on every floor, which sounds opulent but was fairly standard in multinational chain hotels . . . only to go out into the city and see this.

Mumbai has around twenty-two million people living in it, and statistics say that seventy percent of them live in the slums. Living in a slum in Mumbai doesn't mean not being able to get Wi-Fi or struggling to pay off that twenty-five-hundred-square-foot home. And it doesn't mean poorly maintained housing in economically depressed areas. In Mumbai it means having limited access to clean water and food and electricity, not to mention educational opportunities. These slums harbor over seven million children growing up in absolute poverty. Kids who are forced to work at an early age. Kids who have to forget trying to learn simply because they're focused on trying to live.

I had seen some of the staggering numbers on India. How it was estimated to contain one-third of the world's poor. How almost 100,000 people were estimated to die each year from diarrhea—not from the Ebola plague or from war, but simply from bad sanitation.

The ride there overwhelmed Jen and me. We were humbled and immediately reminded to be more grateful for what we have. Most important, we were thrilled to have an opportunity to bring Zoey home.

Once we got to the orphanage, the staff welcomed us with open arms. Apparently they had done some research on us (thank goodness for Google) and knew all about us. The first words out of their mouths were "Where's Will?" While Will wasn't a secret we were keeping from them, we were advised against bringing him with us to the orphanage. But Will's infectious smile reached even to the inner city of Mumbai, and they were disappointed he wasn't there. We explained that we thought it best to be able to focus on Zoey and that William was anxiously anticipating Zoey's return to the hotel so he could meet his baby sister.

First we met with the staff that managed the orphanage. There were a number of women that run the orphanage and women's rescue home. They were very pleasant and generous. After an offering of tea and cookies, they took us for a brief tour of the grounds. We met some of the other children, visited the room where Zoey had spent much of her time over the past two years, and then returned to the front office. A woman not much taller than us walked through the courtyard and into the office carrying a small child. I knew right away it was Zoey.

Those dark eyes stared blankly at everyone in the room right before she began wailing. Zoey cried in the caregiver's arms. Then she cried in Jennifer's arms. She cried as she was carried back to her room for a final "wardrobe change" before she left with us.

This is going to work, I told myself. *We're going to win her over. She'll just take a little longer than Will did.*

I finished up the paperwork and signed the logbooks while Jen extracted as much info about Zoey's history as she could. Our screaming daughter reentered the room, was handed to Jen, and off we went. We climbed back onto the bus and put Zoey in her car seat. She screamed continuously for about ten minutes and then promptly fell asleep.

Deep down, I held on to this hope that Zoey would soon learn not only to know we were there to help her, but that she would love us in the same way we already loved her.

It turned out these things would take a lot of doing, especially in those early days. For a while there, it would seem like it was going to take a miracle for Zoey to accept me.

Watching Will greeting his sister for the first time after we returned to the hotel and introduced the two of them was something we'll never forget. Will was so full of joy and couldn't wait to meet his dear and precious Zoey. When he saw her for the first time, Zoey sat on the couch, giving him a look of absolute terror, and then Will gave her a small kiss on her foot. The simple kind that seemed to say *You're going to be okay, Zoey.*

Jen and I couldn't help becoming teary-eyed watching our little boy greet our little girl. Our family of three had suddenly turned into a foursome. An overwhelming sense of joy filled me as I watched Will and Zoey. We spent that first evening together in the hotel getting to know one another. We played games, got some rest, ate dinner, played more, and finally got the kids to bed. We put Will and Zoey near each other on the far side of our bedroom. Will was on a crib mattress with pillows and blankets all around and his CPAP plugged into the wall. Zoey was but three feet from him in a tiny wood crib with no legs that sat on the floor. They both fell asleep within minutes of each other. Seeing them sleeping together that first night is one of my fondest memories.

I would have to wait to sail off into the sunset because when I woke up the next day I discovered Zoey still didn't want to have anything to do with me. For whatever reason, Zoey decided Daddy was on her list, and not the good list. When Mommy was around, this wasn't that big of a deal, but when Jen stepped away, Zoey would refuse to look at me and pulled away when I tried to hold her. This was totally different from how it had gone when we adopted Will, but we had read and been told that the adoption experience can vary from one child to another. We wanted it to be an easy transition for Zoey, but we were prepared to accept the challenges a family normally experiences at the onset of adoption.

After flying to New Delhi to visit the doctor in order to provide the medical clearance necessary to get a visa for Zoey, Jen revealed she was still bleeding and was worried that it was related to the procedure (D&C) after the nonviable pregnancy. She called some friends back home and they thought she should come home to be treated. She also discovered that, coincidentally, her boss at Texas

Children's Hospital was working at a hospital in New Delhi that day. We decided that she should go get checked out while I handled getting Zoey's medical exam.

Visiting the doctor's office all felt fairly routine since we had just gone through it with Will. But everything changed when we met the doctor in person. He was a very nice man but for some reason he seemed perplexed by Zoey's stature and even more so by mine. As I tried to explain to the doctor what Jennifer and I both felt was the root of Zoey's short stature, I realized how much I missed Jen.

She would know exactly what to say to him.

The doctor said he understood my explanation but he didn't seem willing to accept it. I kept thinking, *Just shut up and get this over with and get out of here.*

So I shut up and let the doctor fill out the required paperwork so we could move along and get back to the U.S. The doctor finished his exam, which ended with a TB test. The results, he said, could be provided within twenty-four to seventy-two hours from the time the test was administered.

As soon as we left the hospital, I called Jennifer to see how she was doing. She said her boss found an ob/gyn for her to see and the doctor gave her medication that would likely arrest the bleeding to a certain degree but recommended she should go back to the States immediately for care, just like her colleagues had suggested. They were concerned that the amount of blood loss Jennifer was experiencing could become life-threatening.

Imagine flying halfway around the world to meet your beautiful daughter for the first time only to be told you had to leave her and the rest of your family behind to go back home?

It wasn't a simple "I have to go—see you guys later" sort of thing. Jen and I went back and forth, talking about the pros and cons of staying and leaving.

Ultimately, after much deliberation, we concluded that it would be best for Jennifer to travel home and seek immediate care rather than risk further complications. At first we thought it would be a good idea to send Will home with Jen, but after much discussion we decided to send Jennifer home with one of the two security personnel we had in India. They would ensure her safe passage back to Houston while I stayed behind with the kids.

It was the toughest decision we had faced as a couple up until that point.

I knew we could only do the best thing for her health and her life. She needed to get home right away. I needed to be there with our two children.

I can do this.

That's what I kept telling myself as we neared the time of her departure.

I have to do this.

Sometimes life gives you no alternative.

SHARE HOPE WITH OTHERS

Jen

Seven months before I had to take that scary trip home alone to see my doctors after first meeting Zoey, I was on another flight full of hope and excitement. All I could picture on that flight was the smiling face of the son we were on our way to meet for the first time. I sat still in the plane seat, glancing over my shoulder to see the peaceful face of my husband, his eyes closed. Somewhere between Alaska and Siberia, Bill fell asleep, leaving me alone to my thoughts and excitement. The twelve-hour flight from San Francisco to Beijing was almost halfway done. This, of course, meant we were halfway there.

I grabbed my phone and took a quick shot of Bill. I wanted to show this to Will. We had already sent the New Day Foster Home, where Will was staying, pictures of us, so this would be just another to add to his photo album. I knew that one day we'd share the story of how we adopted him, filling out the context for each of those first snapshots of his parents.

Bill certainly had a right to be so tired. He had spent so much time getting all the details in place for this adoption to happen. It had been less than a year since we had gotten a call from a woman named Martha who told us there was a child available for international adoption. We hadn't expected it to happen so soon, especially after our journey with surrogacy and dealing with two miscarriages. Now all we had to do was wait for the plane to land and then see our son's beautiful face in person.

My heart felt full, wondering what Will might have been experiencing since he'd seen our pictures for the first time. I wanted him to know how loved he already was by his parents, and for him to know how many people were supporting us on this journey. Not only did we have the support of family and friends, but now we had the support of our fans and viewers. Our film crew was on the plane with us, and they were almost as excited as Bill and me to finally set foot in China and bring Will home.

The joy inside me was no different from that of a pregnant woman being driven to the hospital by her husband after having her water break. We might not have had the opportunity to be there when Will was first born, but we knew he was born to be our son. We not only felt a profound love for him, but also felt privileged to have this gift given to us.

I wondered if he clung on to the hope that we had sent to him, the same one that had brought me many hours of comfort myself.

Along with the pictures of Bill and me, we had wanted to send the foster home many presents but had been told only one small item would be allowed. So naturally, we decided that Will needed a Flying Lion to keep him company until we could bring him home.

We hoped that the Flying Lion would stay by his side even after we first met him. It wasn't as if we would just swoop in and pick him up from his foster home, like a parent might do with his child in day care. Will would have to be moved to an orphanage in Hohhot, the capital of Inner Mongolia and the place he was born. This would be where the adoption would officially take place.

I couldn't wait to hold Will in my arms and show him how much we loved him. I couldn't wait for the opportunity to let him know just how safe and protected he would be with us. Sitting on that plane looking at the picture of Will and imagining him being with us back home, I just couldn't wait to be a Flying Lion in his life—to be a source of hope in his life. To share with him stories about all the operations I had endured and to let him know he wasn't alone. I wanted to let him know it was okay to be afraid and to cry. It was okay to imagine the pain being taken away and to even picture himself one day waking up and no longer being a Little Person.

Whatever came his way, I wanted Will to know that there would be two Flying Lions forever by his side, and that we would do our best in any way we could to stop the crying.

HOPE BRINGS MORE HOPE

Bill

How can she be so strong?

As we prepared for Jen to leave India to go back home, I realized I couldn't remember a time when I didn't love this woman. I had looked up to her and followed her career even before she knew me. I had met her early in my childhood and knew about her during college. I admired her ability to overcome obstacles even before I knew her. It felt like it had taken such a long time for us to finally connect and for me to win her over.

I don't want to lose her now.

Jen certainly didn't give any impression of being scared or worried about her health. All she wanted was to make sure she was leaving with things in order.

"So you have enough diapers?" she asked.

"Check."

"How about medication and instructions for the kids' ears, tummies, noses, and everything else?"

I pointed to the bag. "Check."

"The Power of Attorney for Zoey?"

"Check," I said.

We would need that to complete her adoption. So that was a very big check.

"I have the instructions for the flight team in case anything happens," Jen said.

"Check."

Those were the instructions on how to care for a woman with skeletal dysplasia with a cervical spine fusion on the ride home in the event she became unconscious due to severe blood loss.

Wait—what? What's happening here?

Reality washed over me. We had little information about what was going on with Jen, no "connections" to get things done locally, and we couldn't just leave the country together since Zoey's adoption wasn't official yet.

There was no tear-filled *Sophie's Choice* parting of ways between Jen and her kids. Instead, she kissed them good-bye at the hotel and then gave me a hug after I drove her to the airport. I couldn't believe

I was sending my wife home on a plane without me. This wasn't how we planned it. It was supposed to be all of us going home together, as one happy family.

It would hit me suddenly at two in the morning in the hotel. The kids were asleep and the room was pitch black. I had slipped out of the bed and entered the bathroom to make sure Will and Zoey didn't hear their daddy crying. I wiped tears off my face as I thought about Jen. She was probably somewhere over Afghanistan and headed toward Russian airspace at this very moment. I knew she had to be alone and scared on that plane.

The critical thing was that she needed medical attention. She had been bleeding for days and was becoming weaker with each passing hour. And she'd be eight thousand miles away from help if she'd stayed in India.

As I sat on the edge of the bathtub, sobbing and tracking United Flight 83 from Delhi Airport to Newark International, I couldn't help but begin to lose hope.

I remember making the decision that we were going to leave India by the weekend, which was only a couple of days after Jen left. Everybody around me said this probably wasn't going to happen because of all the things that needed to take place, but I wasn't going to take no for an answer. I couldn't be with my wife, but I could make sure to do everything physically possible to get on a plane and get home to her as soon as I could. So on that Thursday and Friday, that's exactly what I did.

Back at home Jennifer was undergoing a barrage of tests. She had MRIs and CT scans, blood work and examinations. I would get periodic updates, but no actual answers. I decided not to spam her with texts and questions on how she was doing. Her parents were taking care of her and going with her to and from the hospital. Since I wasn't there, she didn't need any sort of commentary from her husband about her prognosis.

After finding the e-tickets for our trip back home in my email inbox, I also discovered a voice mail on my phone from Jennifer, asking me to call. When I spoke to her, any sort of hope I had left inside of me dissipated.

"They discovered it is a choriocarcinoma," Jen told me the same way she would tell a patient the results of her findings. "It's stage three cancer. It's already metastasized to my lungs. It is growing into my uterine wall, which is what was causing all the bleeding."

She told me that choriocarcinoma was a cancer that grows in a woman's uterus and starts in the tissue that normally turns into the placenta. As Jen went through details about what they had done and what the doctors were going to do next, I listened in complete disbelief. I was no longer worried. Now I was devastated. I couldn't believe it. How could this be happening *now*? Right after picking up Zoey!

Some reality shows are desperate for drama, but we just wanted some boredom in our lives. Adding Will to our family had been plenty of excitement, and with Zoey completing our family of four, there was enough going on. But now, with this revelation . . .

I breathed out and shook my head, knowing the truth.

I gave my wife cancer.

And yeah, in a sense—a really awful, morbid sense—this was

exactly what had happened. While we were having fun in the love shack on the beach during our vacation, something happened that didn't just change our plans a bit. This wasn't like the clouds suddenly covering up the sun on the beach. This felt more like a tsunami engulfing everything on the shore and in its way.

Come back to reality, Bill. Jen needs you strong. She can't have one more thing to worry about.

So I tried my best to encourage her and also let her know we would be by her side soon. I couldn't imagine how she felt. I had this ache inside of me and felt the loss of optimism. This was unusual since I've always been optimistic no matter what life has brought. But this situation was unusual, to say the least.

As I packed for our twenty-four-hour excursion home, feeling down, I received a photo from Jen. She was sitting in the hospital bed with her mom on one side and a PICC line catheter dangling from her arm on the other. And for those of you who might not know what a PICC happens to be, let me give you a few details on it.

PICC stands for "peripherally inserted central catheter." It's an IV line with around three feet of thin hose they insert just above your elbow and then snake through your body. The hose is pushed all the way to the main vein next to your heart, called the superior vena cava. A PICC is used when the medication they're giving is extremely dangerous and harmful to smaller veins like the ones in your arm. With the strong medication the doctors would be giving Jen, it would have blown out her arm and the IV.

So yeah—Jen didn't have any ordinary IV in her arm.

Yet the amazing thing in the picture she sent wasn't seeing the PICC in her arm but seeing the smile on her face. I couldn't believe it. She didn't look scared in the least. Jen had the same sort of smile that she wore while we were in Florida frolicking. I knew she was familiar with the PICC since she had put countless ones in infants no bigger than a Double-Double from In-n-Out Burger. But still—after everything that had happened—seeing that grin on her face changed me.

I knew that if they'd taken my picture after I got a PICC I'd be giving them the middle finger.

This amazing and strong woman was actual smiling as she was starting chemotherapy.

I suddenly knew why I felt empty and why my hope was ebbing. It was because in so many different ways, Jen was my hope. She was a living example of it. I had known her courage before we officially met and I knew it even more deeply right now.

If a woman born with skeletal dysplasia who has had more than thirty surgeries in her life and just left her newly adopted daughter along with her husband and son in India only to discover she has stage three cancer could be sitting in a hospital bed with *that* type of smile on her face, then . . .

I knew we were going to fight this thing together. All four of us. We were going to handle this and beat this thing.

In my lifetime, I have met some remarkable people who have inspired me—doctors, business executives, inspirational leaders, bona fide heroes. And while I am thankful for the contributions they have made to help make me who I am today, there is no one braver in my world and no one who instills hope like Jen does. No one has a more positive outlook. Sitting in that bed halfway around the world, hooked up to a machine that would pump poison into her body, she showed me what it looked like to have hope in the midst of terrible circumstances.

WE ALL HAVE A CHOICE

Bill and Jen

We've discovered throughout our lives that hope can come in many forms. It can show up on the face of a doctor like Steven Kopits. It can be held like a stuffed animal named Flying Lion. It can appear in an instant and then be washed away just as quick. It can be lost during a plane flight and restored in a picture. It can be modeled by a loving spouse and magnified by the love you have for your children.

More than anything, we know that hope is indeed a choice. It's the decision to believe that things can and will get better. Hope is more than just confidence or optimism. Having hope means you anticipate a positive outcome, regardless of the circumstances.

Every day we hear from people—many we've never had a chance to meet—how our stories have impacted them and brought hope to their lives. And every day, we encounter people far less fortunate than the two of us. Men and women not blessed with loving families or the skilled hands and heart of a Dr. Kopits in their lives.

We see people battling for their lives and all we can do is share the hope that has been instilled in us. The same sort of hope we're trying to impart in Will and Zoey.

Barbara Kingsolver, a novelist and a poet, once said the following:

"The very least you can do in your life is to figure out what you hope for. And the most you can do is live inside that hope. Not admire it from a distance but live right in it, under its roof."

We certainly believe this to be true.

Sometimes hope comes when you least expect it.

Sometimes hope may seem completely unrealistic.

Sometimes hope shows up in living examples.

Sometimes hope is revealed in yourself.

Sometimes it's only after persisting that hope pays off.

Hope, however, is something you can always choose, and it's something you can live right in, under its roof, anytime you want to.

REMINDERS OF HOPE

1. Make a list of the people in your life who have given you the most hope and encouragement.

2. Print out a picture of each of these people in whatever fashion you can, perhaps as a collage on your phone or as a set of photos to fit a five-by-seven frame.

3. Put the picture someplace where you'll see it daily as a reminder of the hope you've been given.

4. While you're at it, write them a note just to say thanks. Text them a simple THANKS FOR BEING YOU message. Email them. If you're brave enough, use a pen and paper to handwrite a letter and send it in the mail! Believe us, they'll be impressed by that. The point is to thank them for their generosity in your life.

5. Now make another list. This one can just be a list of names without the photos. Make a list of people *you'd* like to inspire. Imagine yourself playing the role of a Dr. Kopits in someone's life. Obviously if you have children, you will add their names. But who else? A friend? A colleague? Make a list and then think of ways that you can bring some joy and light to their lives.

CHAPTER THREE

INITIATE

*"When I have finally decided that a result is worth getting,
I go ahead on it and make trial after trial until it comes."*
—Thomas Edison

EVERY ADVENTURE HAS TO HAVE A STARTING POINT

Jen

My kindergarten graduation was, in some ways, a very important day in my life, because it made me realize two very significant things.

I was only six, but I had already been through a lot. My first surgery occurred when I was two—a cervical spine fusion. My first osteotomy took place when I was three. So many of the kids my age had probably never even been back to the hospital after being born, and most had probably only seen doctors for things like colds and flu bugs and annual checkups. So when I finally realized I had finished kindergarten and was headed to first grade after the summer, a new feeling filled me.

A great sense of accomplishment.

Yes, I realize I was only six, and that pretty much everybody graduates from kindergarten. But after I'd spent most of my life in a cycle of operations and recovery, it felt great to know I had finally completed something. I had accomplished something. I'd gotten through and I'd passed, and I'd done it on my own. Of course I had help, but I was the only one standing on the stage and getting my kindergarten "diploma" from Rolling Hills Elementary.

I knew I could do a lot more if I just kept going.

For every journey, there has to be a starting point, a moment when you begin. At that age, I loved the idea of pretending I was going out on some adventure anytime I headed outside and got on my bike. My favorite game was Dungeons & Dragons, where you guide your hero through a campaign full of magic and surprises. Life, of course, is a journey, but it's often too easy to stay home and refuse the call to adventure. Doing that would have been like picking the player you wanted and creating the character sheet as you prepared to play Dungeons & Dragons, and then never bothering to roll the dice to start.

I didn't realize it at that moment, but my kindergarten graduation would be the start of many educational milestones. The path would certainly be far longer than I would have even dreamed back then, but that's what it takes when you decide to go into the world of medicine. On that day, I just knew that I could indeed get through a year of school. I had enjoyed it. I was proud.

Another reality, however, hit me as well. The way all of us were lined up and walking down the aisle together made me realize something: I was shorter than everybody else.

I hadn't ever really thought long and hard about it until this moment. It wasn't a negative thing—just a fact of life. Everybody standing on the stage next to me was taller than me. This was the first time I really realized I was different, I had dwarfism.

Part of our motto of Thinking Big has been to acknowledge starting points and move on. These points can come as a kindergartner or as a doctor and a wife or as a mother. It doesn't matter, because in any case you have to start with the same mentality.

I've stepped up to the stage and I have my invitation to keep going.

At that graduation, a lot of the kids held that piece of paper and took it to mean "School is finished and now it's summertime!" For me, it said "Let's go, Jennifer!" Sure, I might have been shorter than everybody else, but I was a kindergarten graduate now, ready for anything that might be up the road ahead waiting for me.

INTRODUCE YOURSELF

Bill

"Life all comes down to a few moments. This is one of them."

I could hear the quote from the 1987 movie *Wall Street* going off in my head. A young Charlie Sheen played Bud Fox, an ambitious stockbroker who dreamed of working with a ruthless corporate raider named Gordon Gekko. Bud eventually gets an interview with Gekko after calling him fifty-nine days in a row. He's got this one shot, one opportunity to make an impression on him.

I tried to get comfortable in the hard metal seat I was sitting in and watched a young woman four chairs down from me being called to the desk. I was part of the cattle call here, one of twenty candidates holding a résumé and a job application and ready to have an in-person interview. The number of people applying for the job felt a bit intimidating, but we were all in this room for the same reason.

Getting started is always the tricky part of anything in life, especially when it's something new. The process can always feel a bit daunting. Whether it's getting a job, going to school, or skydiving, nothing new or difficult comes easily. But one thing is always true: The first step—even though it might indeed be one of the toughest—is simply the beginning.

I graduated from New York University in 1996 with a degree in biology. I wasn't quite clear as to what the rest of my life would look like. A degree in biology and little interest in doing bench research meant I had done a lot of studying for a career I had little interest in pursuing.

I moved back home with my mom and began a job search in the pharmaceutical and medical device industry. Most kids who graduated with a degree in biology were doing the same thing in the nineties. It was a lucrative industry to be in at the time, and since I couldn't afford to go back to school for a new degree, I thought it best to pursue a job that would utilize my education.

My foray in the "real world" began inauspiciously. My job search lasted months. I would start by sending out résumés via fax machine, an exercise that nowadays feels a bit like using a rotary dial on a telephone or making a mix tape on a cassette. I would also call numbers from the help-wanted pages and attend job fairs throughout the tri-state area.

I had a pretty stout résumé, filled with degrees and extracurricular activities, so I would receive an interview very regularly. On a rarer occasion I would receive a second interview.

I was excited about the prospect of getting a job. As I said, the pharmaceutical industry was where you wanted to be in the late nineties. A sales rep had all the things a twenty-one-year-old wanted: a great salary and potential of making far beyond that; a car and security and the chance to be considered among the elite in the world of sales. Landing a job like this meant you were truly gifted.

I was a bit nervous, but I didn't question for a second whether or not I was right for this sort of role. I was born with the ability to sell and I knew the medical industry better than pretty much anybody, including some of those working inside it. This is the sort of thing that happens when you grow up inside hospitals. Plus, I made it my goal to know everything I could.

The quote from that movie popping up in my head wasn't unusual. I basically memorize every movie I ever watch. It's almost as if

I have an eidetic memory for useless stuff like movie lines and credit card numbers, though this never seemed to help me in college. It did, however, equip me for the job I was applying for.

When I finally heard my name called, I walked over to the table and handed the man my résumé. I wore my best gray pinstripe suit and a new tie and knew my attire was as impeccable as the sheet of paper I handed to the interviewer. As I shared a little bit about myself, I had no doubt that I was the right person for this job. I knew I was qualified, and my short stature had nothing to do with my ability to excel at the job.

I didn't think there was any sort of elephant in the room. I was capable and qualified and I knew I could fill this role. I wanted him to know how well I knew the medical industry, yet I didn't want to get into too many details right away, appearing to be some sort of know-it-all.

I could have told him I had memorized every bone in the body by the age of eight. I could have explained I understood the pharmaceutical world all too well. Entering that world to sell them was only natural because I knew every product and even had an idea of how it was applied and what the dosing might be. This all came naturally to me because of the exposure I'd had as a patient my whole life. But I wanted to avoid having my stature, by virtue of discussing my medical history as the basis for my industry knowledge, become the subject of the interview.

Even as I shared information about myself and why I was the right fit for the job, I could tell that the interviewer had already made up his mind. It was nothing he actually said, but it was how he said his words. There was a sense of indifference and busyness in his questions, rushing them and then stopping my answers short to simply get another necessary question asked. It was also his expression and body language and the way his eyes moved away from mine onto the other candidates.

I've always felt like I can read people well only moments after meeting them. Over the years, it seems I've become deftly attuned to a person's nonverbal communication. Sometimes this can drive Jen crazy since she's always more willing to give people the benefit of the doubt. Perhaps this was something I had developed over time as a defense mechanism; I could immediately see a person's attitude as they spoke to a Little Person, namely me. Over time, this perspective has changed, and perhaps softened a bit as I've become older. But at the time, it only served to make me more frustrated as the interview progressed.

I look back on initial job interviews like this one, and I realize how I should have addressed the reality of the situation. I should have started things out by saying, "Yes, I was born with skeletal dysplasia but this won't impact my ability to do this job. . . ."

This was something Jen addressed head-on when she had applied to medical school. But in my mind, at this point in my life, I felt like I didn't need to bring it up. I felt like I could stand on my own merits—and they were certainly big enough to make me worth hiring. Another part of me had this me-versus-the-world mentality. I was Rocky Balboa, the underdog boxer about to fight the undisputed World Heavyweight Champion Apollo Creed. And most important, at the time, I was too stubborn to realize that in the real world, what people are supposed to do and what people actually do are sometimes very different.

"If you have nothing else, that will be all," the interviewer said. "Thank you for your time."

The man's handshake felt more like he was nudging me forward, like a kindergarten teacher might do to a child who wasn't leaving the class to go to gym with the rest of his classmates. I knew I had to end the interview with one more attempt to prove my worth.

"This is a great job opportunity and I would really like to work here," I said. "I can do an outstanding job and know I would be a good fit for your team. I would love to set up a time to talk a little more about this."

"We'll be in touch."

His forced grin and his raised eyebrows made me think of the *Saturday Night Live* skit with David Spade and Helen Hunt. They played two rude airline attendants on Total Bastard Airlines. Everybody who walked by them got the same dismissive "Buh-bye" as they exited the plane. They tried to appear friendly but really were just feigning the farewell and not bothering to hide their contempt.

As I walked away from the interview, I knew the only thing I'd hear from the company would be a thanks but no thanks. This was, however, all part of the process.

When you're starting off on a journey, you have to stand up and start walking. If you're headed somewhere far away, you have to climb in the car and start the engine. But part of this process is to always remember it's about the journey and not the destination. It's the experience you need to enjoy, even if you realize you may need to reroute the way you get there.

As I climbed into my car and headed back home, I saw the dismissive expression of the interviewer's face and realized I couldn't let it discourage or define me. All it did was light a fire inside of me to keep going and to keep trying. There were plenty of other job opportunities, and I'd go for them, too.

Another quote from *Wall Street* sounded out in the deep vault of my photographic memory. It was something Gordon Gekko tells Bud Fox as he calls him early one morning with his marching orders.

"This is your wake-up call, pal. Go to work."

That was exactly what I planned to do. But I soon realized that I was going to have to do it my own way. I was going to have to take more initiative if I was going to succeed.

LOOK BENEATH THE SURFACE
- -

Jen

I've had to take the initiative a lot of times in my life, creating opportunities for myself where none seemed to exist, and so I've discovered time and time again that initiating something can and usually does lead to some sort of discovery. For example, there was this time I visited Lost River Cave in Kentucky when I was eight years old.

It was summertime and I was recovering from one of my surgeries that had started off those summer months. While other kids were outside playing, I was rolling around the house in a wheelchair with my leg in a cast. I was grateful to be home in Florida after spending several weeks at the hospital in Maryland, yet I still wished I could have both of my legs free to do whatever I wanted with my friends. Still, there was some good news—one of my best friends was coming back home.

Aunt Chrissy was my mother's youngest sister and was only eleven years older than me. I would become very close to Chrissy. She let me tag along with her everywhere.

Chrissy always felt more like a big sister than an aunt to me. She was a talented artist who loved photography and writing and wanted to go to school to become a journalist. As we grew up together, Aunt Chrissy and I became best friends. That was why it was hard to see her go off to college.

A year later, Chrissy decided to leave the University of Kentucky and come back home. She was a native Floridian like me and the dreary, cold weather was just too much for her. This was when my parents decided to initiate a grand plan. They offered to pick her up and bring her back to Orlando to stay with us for a while. My parents always loved taking trips in the car, so this would be a great excuse to get on the road and explore.

Even though I was still in a bit of pain, I was glad for the change of pace, and I was excited to see Chrissy. My brother, at just two years old, was locked into his car seat. I sat across from him with my leg in a cast, which was also buckled in as if it were a separate passenger sitting between us. As much as I hated sitting in the back of a car, at least it was better than lying around at home waiting for my cast to come off.

By the time I hit eight, I started to become aware of who I was and what life looked like for someone like me. On the outside, I was shorter than everybody else and would stay this way for the rest of my life. I had to endure painful surgeries that broke my bones and left me with scars and stitches. My parents didn't let me go to water parks because I couldn't swim even though all my friends were going. I had taken lots of lessons but no matter how hard I tried, I couldn't tread water or even float. My life, I knew, already looked a lot different from those of my friends.

Life meant missing out on some things, whether it was a trip to the local pool with the kids or a particular ride at Disney World I wasn't allowed on because of my height.

What made things tougher was the fact that I never got to know many of the people I would have otherwise been around. My surgeries and the recovery time often meant I wasn't around to play or even get to know the neighbors. I missed out on birthday parties and sleepovers and playdates.

It might have been easy to believe that my short stature and the surgeries and the missing out defined me. That this was all that would exist in my life.

It was helpful to have an aunt and sister and best friend like Chrissy. She was always encouraging me. "No one person or situation can make you happy or sad," Aunt Chrissy said. "We get to choose how we feel."

That had always made sense to me, and I couldn't wait to have my best friend back in my life.

As we drove past the sprawling green lawns and redbrick buildings of the University of Kentucky's campus to pick her up, I could barely contain my excitement. I bounced up and down in my seat as my mom checked the campus map and Dad navigated the narrow streets that threaded through the campus. When we finally pulled up in front of her dorm, Chrissy ran out the front door and straight to the car, hugged my parents, and joyfully hopped in the backseat to connect with, I can only assume, her favorite niece. My cast had to rest in her lap, but she didn't seem to mind and neither did I. In fact, my cast was a great way to pass the time. She doodled all over it with Magic Markers.

With our mission of picking up Aunt Chrissy accomplished, my parents decided to go ahead and make a vacation out of it. We planned to stop at some tourist attractions on the way home. My dad started driving while I updated Chrissy on all the events she had missed. Mostly, we talked about school, my surgery, and how much I missed the beach. I wouldn't be able to go until I got my cast off in two weeks and went through physical therapy.

Back then, there were no smartphones or GPS built into your car. Dad had to rely on his sense of direction and countless maps from Rand McNally. Before long, we reached our first waypoint in the trip. There are a number of caverns in the Kentucky-Tennessee area you can visit. We stopped at one called Ruby Falls, just outside of Chattanooga. We paid for our tickets and went inside. The walls of the cavern are huge, and they are carved with these intricate patterns from thousands of years of water flowing past the rocks. There is a dramatic waterfall through a tunnel of rock that they highlight with colored lights.

I couldn't believe something so immense and incredible was hidden inside the earth. Such beauty that could have gone undiscovered and unnoticed. Now, we were able to look at it and celebrate the natural artwork of the world.

Soon after this, we visited the Lost River Cave, which was located just outside of Bowling Green, Kentucky. The tour we took included a boat ride across an underground lake. As you might imagine, I was terrified at first. Remember, I couldn't swim, and I couldn't help but think my heavy cast would make a perfect anchor if I were to fall out of the boat. As we entered the mammoth entrance to the cave and headed down a flight of stairs to climb into the metal boat, I pictured my imminent death. As they helped me into the boat, I felt it move back and forth, and I felt terror. My parents, however, seemed more confident that the experience outweighed any unlikely risk of me sinking to the bottom with my cast.

Of course, my mom and dad were right.

I've been a science geek for as long as I can remember. Going to these caves gave me a chance to see and feel a lot of what I had read about in school. Stalactites and stalagmites were everywhere. The air was stagnant and it was so humid that the cave walls looked like they were sweating. As we rode in what Ripley's Believe It or Not! claimed to be the shortest and deepest river in the world, we learned about cave formations and their wildlife.

I also learned something else. With my parents and my brother and Aunt Chrissy surrounding me on the boat that waded through this complex and magnificent cave hidden away in the hills of Kentucky, I discovered that there was always more beneath anything than what you could see. The surface did not and could not define you. From the outside, this just looked like any other hill. You could pass it every day and never have a clue about the majesty and the mystery that lay underneath.

There's more to anything in life than what you see. But you have to decide to step out and discover it.

I, for one, didn't want to miss out on moments like this. I chose to take the initiative to always try to see the hidden depths in everyone I met and everything I adventured to do. I still have to remind myself that hidden beauty can lie beneath the most mundane hills that we traverse every day.

GO ABOVE AND BEYOND

Bill

I could barely hear the ringing phone over the wind and the snow outside my house. It was a cold weekend in February 2003, and a nor'easter was bearing down on Long Island. I picked up the phone, not expecting the news I would get from the person on the other end of the line.

"Hey, Bill. How's the weather up by you?"

It was Fred, the IT director from our corporate office in Pennsauken, New Jersey. I had come a long way from those initial job interviews, and after going through more than fifty of them, I had finally landed a job with a medical device distribution company. Our target market included alternate-site infusion pharmacies and hospitals. We sold a range of products, including pharmaceuticals, durable medical equipment, and medical supplies.

It was a great place to start. I learned a lot from my bosses, my clients, and my coworkers. And because I took a lot of pride in the work I did, I quickly became an expert. I knew more details about the sixteen thousand–plus items we sold than anyone else in the company. I developed great relationships with my customers and, after a short tenure, was promoted into management. After just a few years with the company, we had grown to nearly $60 million in annual revenue.

The company then merged with three other organizations to become a conglomerate. This organizational restructure, which took place in 1999, lasted a very short period of time before we were acquired. The new owner, a company called Mediq, Inc., dissolved the conglomerate, spinning off two of the four entities and merging the other two under their corporate structure.

What none of us realized at the time was that our new owner had a terrible track record and was known for poorly integrating their acquisitions. We were the last of many companies to be acquired before the organization filed for bankruptcy.

The disruption, from the top down, was tremendous. The workforce was reduced by one-third in less than a month. Our revenues tumbled to nearly fifty percent of what they had been the year before. But during this disappointing time in the company's evolution, there was also opportunity. The management team that ran the smaller company I was originally hired to work with was promoted to turn around the organization and find a buyer. That meant I would receive another promotion, an increase in pay, and would be responsible for millions of dollars in growth as we cleaned up the company and positioned it for sale.

Now, at this point I was feeling pretty good about my situation. I had worked hard and became an integral part of the company. I was a good salesman, a fair manager, and I liked the work I did. However, like many of the people employed by the company that had just filed bankruptcy, I was unsure of my future.

And now, our IT manager was calling me on a Sunday . . . in the middle of a snowstorm.

"I haven't even bothered shoveling my sidewalk yet," I told him as we chatted for a few moments.

"I've got some news," Fred said in a matter-of-fact tone. "The company is letting me go. My final day is next Friday."

I wasn't shocked by the news because of all the turmoil and turnover in the company over the last year.

"Look, one of the last things I need to do before I can get my severance package," the IT director said, "is bring you the operating system and install it at your office."

I could only laugh. "Like now? Today?"

The corporate office was two and a half hours away from me. Driving to Long Island would be a nightmare.

"I don't have a choice," Fred said.

I realized the obvious.

Neither did I.

"Okay. Can you pick me up? My little sports car will never make it in this snow. Just let me know when you get close."

I looked out the window and saw a world full of white. The last thing I wanted was to head out into the snow to go to work and do something I wasn't even good at. But going with the flow and dealing with the unexpected was something I was accustomed to. Something I specialized in. And it had gotten me this far in the company and ultimately in my career.

Hearing about Fred's termination wasn't a surprise, yet discovering he needed to hand-deliver the company's operating system to me was quite a shock. He would be installing it in the closet next to my office and then teaching me how to turn it on and off. To say I needed teaching was an understatement. I didn't even own a computer in college (we had computer labs back then). I definitely was not the most confident computer geek. I was, however, a good employee, so I ventured out into the frozen tundra to do my job.

I waded through the twenty inches of snow that had fallen and made it to the curb, where I met Fred waiting in the company car provided to him for the journey, a big Chevy Suburban, to give me a ride to the office. I greeted him and avoided talking much about him being let go. A quote from Miracle Max from my favorite movie, *The Princess Bride*, warned me to be quiet: "The King's stinking son fired me, and thank you so much for bringing up such a painful subject."

With all the fresh snow surrounding us, we literally had to shovel our way to the door of the building. In the back of his SUV were two monitors, a large computer tower, a printer, and lots of wires. Basically, these were the keys to the kingdom he was handing me. The only thing was, he needed to show me how to properly insert the keys into the necessary doors in order to open them.

We cleared a space in the computer closet and carried everything in. After setting up the system and connecting all the wires, I received a ten-minute overview on how the system works and was handed the manual. That was it.

"I'm done—my last task."

After dropping me back off at my apartment, Fred turned the corner, back into the blizzard, and left. I couldn't help wondering when I might be in the same situation.

Miracle Max's voice could be heard again: "While you're at it, why don't you give me a nice paper cut and pour lemon juice on it? We're closed."

Ah, my amazing memory. If only I could use it for fame and fortune instead of funny quotes. Yet . . . I knew that I was a fast learner, and I knew that brain of mine came in handy when necessary. This was one of those moments.

Should I simply stay home and slip into an oversized Giants sweatshirt and spend the rest of the day eating junk food and watching ESPN? That was a nice thought, but it was also a ridiculous one. I knew if we wanted to do business on that coming Tuesday (we had closed the office Monday because of the blizzard), I would need to learn a lot more than I knew at that moment. So I waited until the storm subsided and shoveled my way to my car. After slipping and sliding out of my apartment complex parking lot, I went down to the nearby 7-Eleven and got two cups of coffee and returned to the office to learn about our system. The ride was a bit precarious but I made it.

I don't know what came over me. I wasn't particularly interested in taking on this new task. I wasn't promised anything, and frankly I wasn't paid nearly enough to take on any new responsibilities. Most people probably would have done the sensible thing and stayed home, leaving the worry back at the office to deal with on Tuesday morning.

But taking the initiative means working on something right away, even if it happens to be during a blizzard on a Sunday afternoon. It means getting off the couch and going to solve a problem and then working at it until you're finished.

As I've gotten older, I've realized that I've always been the kind of person who takes the initiative without being told what to do. I've always enjoyed challenges—those are the things that have driven me to work hard. As I worked in my office with the two monitors and the mammoth computer tower, trying to figure out how to make sense of it, I wasn't thinking about what it would do for my career. I didn't think anything of it and accepted the challenge and decided to go ahead and get it done.

I had no idea it would end up making me irreplaceable as the company was marketed to potential suitors.

Several months later, I would discover this reality when I got a call in the office.

"Bill, would you mind coming to the conference room, please?"

This is one of my fondest memories of this transitory, tenuous period of working for the company. The broker who was working on hopefully luring an investor to buy our company had come to our offices that day for a meeting with senior staff. I wasn't initially part of that meeting until getting that call. After I walked into the conference room and sat down, I was greeted with a barrage of questions related to the company's performance. It turned out that every financial and sales report the business broker needed to facilitate the company's sale would have to be created by none other than yours truly.

If for no other reason than the fact that everyone else in IT had already been dismissed, I became the single person with the keys to the store. Thankfully, I wasn't the only person to notice how valuable I had become to this process.

My boss used to say to me, "Stay focused on the task at hand. Eventually, the money comes." When he first said that I thought he was crazy. It's easy for a guy who's made a decent chunk of change to say that sort of nonsense. But he was right. Sometimes when you take the initiative, you are rewarded down the road in ways you never expected. This was one of those cases.

As the "book" was created to posture the company for sale, I was provided with compensation in exchange for my participation in facilitating any requests from potential purchasers. It was my first "golden parachute." We would finally find two different companies to acquire the two divisions as separate transactions. Our parent company was acquired by Hill-Rom, and the business I had a large part in growing was acquired by Invacare Corporation.

I should have been compensated doubly for my efforts, don't you think?

Once the dust settled, much of my management team, including many of my bosses and mentors, had been let go.

There I was, a single person who knew both the business and the IT side of things, suddenly solely responsible for a smooth transition and handoff to the new company. As promised, I seamlessly integrated our revenue, operating system, and sales data into the parent company's infrastructure. In fact, I did such a good job that I was no longer needed and became one of the many people who lost their job as part of the acquisition.

Thanks and buh-bye. Wait . . . was it the buh or the bye you didn't hear? Buh-bye.

Sure, most people would be kicking themselves in the rear at this point. Why didn't I extend my stay or drag my feet or be less cooperative in order to do everything I could to keep my job as long as possible? The reason was simple. I might not have been a big fan of my new bosses, but I didn't know how to do any less than my best.

The good news was that while this chapter of my life was concluding—pending successfully winding down the business operations in New York without any sort of drama or catastrophic employee events—I would soon embark on a new career path.

So it was June 2005. Most of the staff was doing well. Most had found new jobs. Some were still looking and a few had decided to take some time off. Meanwhile, I had been in constant contact with my former CEO, Mike Sperduti. He had been working on brokering the sale of an infusion-tubing manufacturer for the past twelve months. I had been working with him when

I could, and we had been discussing general business ideas after work when we would meet at Pace's Steakhouse, a favorite watering hole of ours.

I was trying to figure out what my next move might be. I had been looking around for some time, not exactly sure what I wanted to do next. I didn't really like working for a big corporation, but I wasn't sure if working for myself was the right decision, either. So I took counsel from Michael. He revealed to me that his brokering deal had fallen through and he, too, was looking for the next big thing.

We took the weekend off, enjoying the Fourth of July with our respective family and friends. The following Monday, we spoke on the phone and conceived the idea for creating a business together. It would be our first endeavor, both individually and as partners, into entrepreneurship.

The idea was simple. We would take all of the skills we developed in our previous careers and create a sales consulting business. Our goal would be to aid companies with their growth and development, utilizing the tools, skills, and mind-set that helped us create the success our previous companies had enjoyed under our management.

Initiative looks a little like this. It's reaching out to contacts to inquire about other opportunities. It's easy to put off taking that first step, or to avoid doing it altogether, because of busyness or procrastination or the things that happen in life. But I took that first step; I reached out and produced an idea, which then produced something very tangible. A consulting business was born.

We began taking on new customers as early as August of that year, just days after we officially incorporated as Emerge Sales, Inc. By the time the holidays rolled around, we had a two-room office built in my house. By the following summer, we had nine people working for us. We knew we were getting too big for my home when the street and driveway looked like a used-car lot. I made the executive decision for us to find new office space when I found one of our employees taking his lunch break on my living room couch, eating a block of cheese from my refrigerator!

Becoming an entrepreneur was the smartest, best decision I ever made. If I hadn't taken the initiative to become a more important part of my former company's transition, I would never have gained the experience and confidence necessary to embark on a journey toward entrepreneurship. Being a creator of business has afforded me a great lifestyle. It has also meant I've created jobs for people. I've seen people buy their first house while working for me. I've seen people start families and buy their first cars. I've also seen companies grow and salespeople get promoted thanks to the work my company provided to theirs.

It took initiative to go get that first job out of college. It took initiative to take on responsibilities that weren't delegated to me. And it took initiative to create a business where none previously existed. That initiative has provided me with immeasurable returns. It has provided me with a sense of confidence and self-worth. Most importantly, that sense of initiative has afforded me the chance to realize many wonderful relationships and experiences I would likely never have experienced otherwise.

MAKE A PLAN—AND THEN TAKE THE FIRST STEP

Jen

"I feel like I need to eventually slow down and act like a twenty-year-old," I said, taking a sip of wine. "Then I realize I'm thirty-one years old and somehow missed my twenties."

My best friend, Lakshmi, could only laugh and then raise her wineglass to make a toast. We sat at a table late on a Friday night after a busy week. A busy week to end a busy month. To be honest, I couldn't remember when life had *not* been a blurry whirlwind.

"I feel like I'd eventually like to settle down and start a family," Lakshmi said.

I agreed . . . what happened to our twenties? Well, I knew . . . medical school, residency, 110-plus-hour-long workweeks.

We didn't intend to spend the evening bemoaning our singleness and tiredness. We had gotten together to have a nice dinner, and instead found ourselves lamenting our situation. We were overworked and underloved and seriously needed to get out more. We needed to experiment with this thing others talked about all the time: *dating*.

"I have a hard enough time trying to pay my bills," I told her. "Not because I can't afford to, but because I never have the time to open them up. I can't imagine what the world of dating would even look like."

I was living in Pittsburgh at the time, working on my neonatal-perinatal fellowship at Magee-Womens Hospital of UPMC (University of Pittsburgh Medical Center). A hundred-hour workweek was typical.

"We have to do something about this," my friend told me. "Weren't we sitting in this exact restaurant a couple of years ago talking about the same thing?"

"Why can I get so much done at the hospital and then leave and get absolutely nothing accomplished at home?" I asked.

Then Lakshmi said something that sounded so perfect it should have been written for a television show.

"Nothing is turning out the way I thought it would. It's like I don't even recognize my life."

I smiled and gave her a nod, then gave her an equally awesome reply. "There's an upside to free falling," I said. "It's the chance you give your friends to catch you."

This was very true. But I have to admit something—these lines were not something she or I actually said. They were favorites from *Grey's Anatomy*. Even though we might have felt them, we never did actually utter them. But I was Meredith Grey and she was Cristina Yang and we were BFFs and soon I'd be hugging her and telling her she's my person.

Our conversation was serious, however, and we were a bit down about the state of our love lives. I eventually made a joke about a website I had signed up for a few months earlier. It was called DateALittle.com and it was geared toward helping Little People connect. Since Lakshmi isn't a Little Person, she was signed up for Match.com.

So we decided to initiate a plan. We each had to email a guy. *That night.*

I'm not sure who had the idea first. I know both of us had some skepticism about going online to find romance. But this was the night when we promised each other that we'd try. It wouldn't be hard: simply reach out to someone who looked interesting. We didn't have to meet them face-to-face. It was just a stranger sending another stranger a greeting.

Signing up on DateALittle.com months before had been easy. But actually having action steps and a plan after doing that—that was a whole other thing. The busyness of my life wasn't going away anytime soon. I had carefully picked out a cute picture of myself and filled out my profile and then made it active and live. But that was as far as I got.

As we shared in our first book, Bill discovered that very profile and sent me a message on it. When I didn't respond, he assumed I was ignoring it and was not interested. Little did he know then I just hadn't bothered to pay my registration fee. Without paying for a monthly subscription you can't access your inbox of messages. It would take this night with my best friend to finally get me to pay up and get active on the dating site.

After logging in, I spent time checking out the various profiles. I was looking for young men my age with good jobs who weren't "married and looking for love." And they had to be people I didn't already know. One turned out to be quite intriguing. A handsome young man named Bill Klein. He had a charming and confident smile, beautiful blue eyes, and had done quite well for himself in the business world. His profile made it seem like he had a good sense of humor, too.

So I decided to put my heart on the line and reveal it all when I sent him the following message:

"Hello! Have we ever met before at a National Little People of America conference? You look familiar."

Yes. That's exactly what I wrote to Bill. I was ninety-nine percent confident we hadn't met at the conference and I was one hundred percent certain this was a terrible pickup line. Perhaps he would see the humor in it and reply. Bill did reply, saying he hadn't been to the convention since he was a kid and never to a national convention, but he'd still love to talk with me.

The rest, as they say, is history. A history that we shared more details about in our first book, *Life Is Short (No Pun Intended)*. If you're interested in more of the details, you can check them out there.

Of course, in that book, I left out the parts about the surgery to remove the grenade from someone's abdomen and the hospital shooting and the plane crash since those stories sound so over-the-top. I also didn't share the first wedding Bill and I planned but had to give up to one of our dying friends who decided to get married there instead. Nobody knows that Bill and I actually wrote our vows on Post-it notes.

Okay, fine . . . That wasn't my life. A girl can be working over a hundred hours a week and be underpaid and have no time to pay the bills and definitely have no time to pursue love, but . . . she can always allow herself one hour a week to watch *Grey's Anatomy*.

And sometimes she also has to take a chance. To make a choice. To go ahead and decide to do something. As Meredith Grey said, "Sometimes, the key to making progress is to recognize how to take that very first step. Then you start your journey."

That journey has continued almost ten years later. And our lives continue to get better and more fascinating and more fulfilling than any television show could ever be, except maybe that one on TLC about that couple in Houston . . .

AND THEN TAKE THE NEXT STEP

Bill

Think of all the incredible inventions that we use every day—every morning, even. We wake up and head to the kitchen and turn on a coffeemaker. (Here's a fun fact for the next time you're on *Jeopardy!*: Edmund Abel Jr. owns the 1971 patent for the automatic drip brewer. *Thank you very much, Edmund.*)

We open our fridge and pull out the milk as we turn on the TV to watch the morning news. We use soap in the showers and put on clothes made of high-tech fibers. We check our email on our laptops or our smartphones before heading out and climbing in our vehicles to drive to work. We listen to the regular radio or satellite radio or have music coming from the Bluetooth connection with our phones.

The list goes on and on and on. There are some things that are hard to imagine living without. Phones, for instance. I have used phones for both earning a living and for conducting research. They also let me stay in touch with people I care about (though I don't particularly like that it's become somewhat of a lost art to converse on the phone instead of texting).

Then there are some things that . . . well, let's be honest. Maybe the world would be a little better off without twist ties, hampers, and golf, just to name a few.

All of us live in a world that's made up of items invented after someone asked: "What if?"

People often like to highlight those two words, and they are certainly powerful. But the true magic comes from the answer: "Let me find out."

Anybody can ask "What if?" Few people will take the time and the energy to go ahead and answer it.

What if I could bring my coffee to work and keep it warm?

What if I wanted to add a flavor to my coffee?

What if I could have a coffeemaker waiting for me at my office that can serve me any kind of coffee imaginable in a single-serving size?

What if I suddenly realize I need an intervention from all the coffee I'm drinking?

The first step is asking that question. Actually, the first step is likely toward the bathroom after drinking all of that coffee! But the most important thing is then doing something about it and trying to solve it. A recent example of this came from an invention I created.

Not that long ago, while Jen and I were still living in an apartment, I noticed something that was rather discouraging. My awesome little dog, Rocky, whom I didn't train very well, was marking everything. He would lift his leg and pee on a person if they stood still long enough. Since I was working out of my home office, I had a chance to see this behavior in action. So I did what any responsible pet owner with seemingly more important things to do than to train my dog would have done. I bought a package of pee pads. I placed a pad on the floor near where he had done some damage before, figuring he would return to the scene of the crime. Indeed, it didn't take too long for him to discover this new target and proceed to micturate on it.

For a moment, I was thrilled that the problem had been solved. Then I realized that Rocky hadn't shut off his hose until walking off of the pee pad and made a Z-shaped line on the floor as he fled the scene. Rocky was unaware of his place in space.

I disregarded this issue, for the most part, and instead walked Rocky as often as possible. It was a decent cure to the problem, unless I was traveling. Jen was uncomfortable walking the dog in dark corners of our apartment complex, so that didn't work so well. Finally, we moved into a house and we were free from having to walk Rocky, since we could just let him out.

"Out, Rock!" we would call to him. He would come scampering in from the other room where he slept much of the day. He might look like a dog, but he acts like a cat. What we learned, though, was that while Rocky loved the outdoors, he didn't like going to the restroom out there. So, he would run outside, bark, play, and chase small woodland creatures and return to the house to pee inside! This was not working out the way we had planned.

We went back to walking him, letting him out, and putting

down a pee pad that would capture some, but not all, of the urine. Fast-forward a bit. I had opened a pet store in Houston but my dog was still having his "issue" and it had continued to go unresolved. I was dragging another chair to the garage to steam clean its wooden leg and it got me thinking. What if I could give him a target he would like to aim for? And my invention was born.

I shared the creation with my brother Joe and his wife, Karen. We put our heads together and devised a way for a pee pad to be opened and, in the process, erect a projection from its center. A three-dimensional target.

We made a prototype and placed it in the middle of the room Rocky was sleeping in that day. Day one, I made the mistake of letting Rocky outside and he decided to go to the bathroom outdoors. The next day, I refrained from letting him out. I needed to see if he would use the new pee pad, or look for other inspiration. Joe and I went to lunch and, upon our return, found the pee pad had been used. Rocky urinated right in the middle of the pad, using the target as his way of understanding his spatial awareness.

I am thrilled to say we are now developing the product and have a patent pending for its unique design. We are hopeful it will turn into something amazing, and it may. Of course, it may fall flat on its face, too. The most exciting part about this isn't that we had an awesome idea. Ideas come and go all the time. It's that we actually took the next step toward making it a reality. Maybe we will have invented the better lightbulb of pee pads, but even if we don't, the point is that we took initiative, and that's the most important step in succeeding.

SHOW UP AND KNOCK

- -

Jen and Bill

Thomas Edison made one or two cool inventions in his lifetime, too. But the best thing he did, in our opinion, is write a whole book full of profound quotes. In fact, it was quite difficult to pick just one with which to start off our chapter. Most of us have heard one of the following:

"Genius is one percent inspiration and ninety-nine percent perspiration. . . ."

This is a clever way of saying ideas are nice but hard work is necessary.

"I have not failed. I've just found ten thousand ways that won't work."

This is encouragement to go ahead and start (a.k.a. *initiate*). And it's a great way to put discouragement in a whole new light (see what I did there?).

We have both taken different journeys in our careers. Both roads we've traveled have been long and interesting and provided lots of surprises along the way. Even when we've both tried to look ahead, knowing what we're good at and what we love to do, there have still been doors that have unexpectedly opened and shut. But the first step, for both of us, was being willing to walk up to that doorstep.

Becoming the medical director of Pediatric Simulation Center at Texas Children's Hospital? How did that happen?

It began by reaching the ladder and starting to climb, one rung after another.

Being a senior manager and an entrepreneur and helping hundreds of companies in my, reasonably speaking, brief career? How did that happen?

It began by showing up. Then showing up when you didn't have to show up. Then doing even more. We have both felt that we needed to be doing more than everybody else in order to prove our worthiness. To quote Stinger (the bald aircraft carrier captain) from *Top Gun,* "You need to be doing it better and cleaner than the other guy." And so that's what we've learned to do. It doesn't always come naturally. We aren't always the best at it, but if we give it everything we've got, one hundred percent of the time, we never go home feeling like we left an opportunity on the table.

We work hard. So hard that sometimes people ask us, *So wait a minute, how can she be a doctor and he be an entrepreneur when they're both . . . reality TV stars and parents at the same time?*

Honestly, it's really, really difficult to juggle everything. And we sometimes drop the ball. We have learned to prioritize things based on what's important to us. And as we add to our plate, our priorities also continue to change. It used to be career above all. Then love entered the picture. Soon after, it was love, career, and television show. Then we became parents and everything changed. Our children became the most important people in our lives, permanently. Our relationship continues to be important because we love each other and need to depend on each other for support, too. Work is important, but less than what it was five, ten, or fifteen years ago. And television, while important, is something we know is fleeting. So we do what we can to enjoy it while it's here, spread our message when appropriate, and plan for its eventual end by not making our lives dependent on it.

But we both think that everyone has potential inside them. Unfortunately many people can't see this. They've been taught to impose labels on themselves, or have had labels imposed on them.

We have both faced a lot of prejudice and hardships and false preconceptions in our lives, and while we know better than that, we, too, are guilty of being labeled and believing those labels to be true. Over time, we have learned that none of this is related to the measure of what you can or can't do.

The first thing you have to do is to flip that switch that says you can't and believe you can—no matter what the obstacles are. Take that first step.

And then take the next one.

Don't wait for someone to tell you it's all right, or to show you the path to walk down. Make your own path. Keep walking. You can do this.

All it takes is a little belief in yourself and a lot of initiative.

INITIATIVE PLAYLIST

(a.k.a. a list of songs to get you going to wherever you need to be)

Set Your Alarm Clock and Wake Up To: "Mr. Blue Sky" by Electric Light Orchestra

Song to Sip Your Morning Coffee To: "Lovely Day" by Bill Withers

If You're Worried About the Upcoming Day: "Happy" by Pharrell

To Play for Your Loved One: "You Make My Dreams" by Daryl Hall & John Oates

For Getting Pumped Before Your Big Moment: "Maniac" by Michael Sembello (for the ladies) and "Start Me Up" by The Rolling Stones (for the guys)

When You Need Motivation to Just Do It: "Jump" by Van Halen

To Blast in Your Car and Let Them Know You're There: "Back in Black" by AC/DC

If You Have Children Who Are Driving You Crazy: "Orinoco Flow" by Enya (to be listened to with noise-reducing headphones only)

When Beginning Any Monstrous Project: The Indiana Jones theme by John Williams

To Feel Good and Get Going: "Yellow" by Coldplay

Go Ahead and Get It Out of Your System: "Smells Like Teen Spirit" by Nirvana

Getting the Girls Together: "Run the World (Girls)" by Beyoncé

Boys' Night Out: "Old Time Rock & Roll" by Bob Seger

When You Decide to Go Ahead and Create Something as Big as Facebook: "In Motion" by Trent Reznor and Atticus Ross

When You Feel Like You Don't Get Enough—: "Respect" by Aretha Franklin

When You Don't Get That Job: "I Won't Back Down" by Tom Petty

When You're Having a *Grey's Anatomy* Moment: "Chasing Cars" by Snow Patrol

For a Toast and a Slow Dance at the End of a Very Long Journey: "I See Fire" by Ed Sheeran

For That Dark Night of the Soul: "Bridge Over Troubled Water" by Simon and Garfunkel

And for the Morning After: "Three Little Birds" by Bob Marley

Another Step Forward: "Brand New Day" by Sting

Just Because You Can: "Safety Dance" by Men Without Hats

CHAPTER FOUR

NO

"A 'No' uttered from the deepest conviction is better than a 'Yes' merely uttered to please, or worse, to avoid trouble."
—Mahatma Gandhi

ASK EVEN IF YOU KNOW THE ANSWER

Bill

Life often comes down to a series of tests that you can pass or fail: critical moments where a family member or a friend needs your advice. A business venture that will make or break your company. A game-tying forty-eight-yard field goal attempt with 6:38 left in overtime when you've already set a franchise record for making twenty-nine consecutive ones. Okay, that last one may not have technically happened to me.

The thing with life is that it has this crazy way of surprising you. Sometimes you can surprise yourself by saying just the right thing to your wife. Perhaps the gamble you take on a new enterprise pays off in ways you wouldn't have dreamed.

But sometimes it doesn't work out the way you hope. Maybe you kick a football and instantly know you've missed. You don't need to watch it trail left, and you don't need to stick around to witness half the fans in MetLife Stadium celebrate the Jets victory while the other half curse you and the rest of the Giants. You know how this is going to turn out without waiting to see it yourself.

I'm not bitter about the Giants' loss to the Jets on December 6, 2015. Nor can I say anything bad about Josh Brown's incredible kicking season. I'm just using it for an illustration. (Okay, maybe I'm still a little hurt, but that's okay because we'll win our fifth Vince Lombardi Trophy next year. #ibelieveineli)

The Yes Moments of life are so much better than the No Moments, aren't they? Tests can come our way as adults that we don't even realize are truly tests until we get graded on them. Yet growing up, tests are an unfortunate reality, and one I never minded since I usually do pretty well on them.

I remember one set of tests that came my junior year of high school where I not only surprised myself, but also the adults giving me the test. The exam consisted of ten shorter tests given over three hours. Before we began, the teacher allowed us to go through some practice questions. We were given instructions on what to do and how long we had with each test. The subjects the tests covered included word knowledge, arithmetic reasoning, science, paragraph comprehension, numerical operations, mathematics knowledge, mechanical comprehension, and electronics info. So basically, if you do really well on the test, you're brilliant and should be paid just for being smart.

As it turned out, I scored in the top one percent of students taking this test. I ended up doing so well that I actually received a call at home from the people who had created this test. They wanted to meet with me—Bill Klein—to talk about my future. I, of course, knew who they were and what this all meant. I was no dummy, remember (see the previous paragraph). When they offered to meet me at Seaport Diner, I jumped at the chance. I wasn't going to say no to a free meal at Seaport Diner.

I showed up early excited for my dinner and curious about the conversation that would take place. I spotted the two men coming to interview me the moment they walked into the diner. When two United States Marines step foot into a restaurant decked out in their dress uniforms, everyone notices. I sat at a table facing them, the only person sitting by himself. And the only teenager in the diner this evening.

The Marines talked to the hostess and obviously mentioned they were meeting a high school kid for dinner. A very *bright* high school kid, I hope they added. She pointed in my direction and they headed over to my table. I smiled at the soldiers as they approached me, and I continued to smile as they passed right on by.

I watched them continue to walk to the back of the restaurant, then get to the back wall and appear confused.

They literally walked right by me. Wonderful.

As they came back to my table, they had confusion all over their faces. Forty-something-year-old Bill Klein would have gotten off his chair to greet them with a confident grin and maybe even a joke. But I was in high school, and I suddenly felt very small. Pun intended.

"Are you Bill Klein?" one of the Marines asked.

They already knew I was, however, and they already were counting down the seconds until they could head back to their base.

I had taken the Armed Services Vocational Aptitude Battery test, which was cleverly called ASVAB. The score students received determined whether they were qualified to enlist in the military. The level of score you got would show your qualifications for being considered for certain specialties and receiving bonuses. A high score like the kind I got improved your chances of getting the job and signing bonus you wanted.

Unless, of course, you were someone with a disability.

The U.S. Marine Corps obviously has very stringent standards for enlistment. When my test results showed up, they called my guidance counselor right away. They wanted me, and they wanted to talk to me about my future.

But then, as soon as they met me, the enthusiastic YES turned straight to a definitive NO in a heartbeat.

I knew the reality. My father had proudly served our country in Vietnam in the seventies, so I knew a little bit about the military. I understood one of the very first rules about joining the Armed Services: You have to complete basic training in order to join. And there were a few problems that would lie ahead of me if I had gone down that road.

The Marines I spoke to basically summed this up in a short and not-so-sweet manner. One of those thanks-but-no-thanks sort of situations.

Great job on the scores, Bill! Come see us on the big screen when the next war movie comes to your local movie theater.

This wasn't the first time I'd received an obvious no, and it would definitely not be the last. At the time, I was disappointed—and angry—but I eventually came to see that the loss wasn't mine, but theirs. While they may have closed the door on my entrance into a career in the military, it wouldn't be the end of my chance to have a career.

In fact, it wouldn't be the last of my involvement with the military. Just a few years ago, I was invited to speak at the Naval Surface Warfare Center in Panama City, Florida. Ironically, the topic was "Inclusion of people with disabilities in the military."

And, hey. At least they paid for my cheeseburger deluxe with fries that night in the diner.

DREAMS DON'T DIE, THEY CHANGE

Jen

It's always fun to ask children what they want to be when they grow up. Sometimes one of them will tell me they want to be a doctor. Maybe they'll come up with something funny, like wanting to build a time machine or become a secret agent or own a zoo or one day become Santa. It's good to encourage dreams—at least within reason. Dreams are good things to have even if you will eventually discover you're not going to be the next Taylor Swift.

When I was young, I wanted to be Jacques Cousteau. I grew up enamored by the French undersea explorer who not only invented the self-contained underwater breathing apparatus (also known as scuba) but who awakened the world to the treasures of the ocean through the programs he produced and wrote for television. I can recall watching many episodes of *The Undersea World of Jacques Cousteau*. The Frenchman was also a talented photographer and writer and inventor.

If someone had asked Cousteau as a child what he wanted to be when he grew up, they probably wouldn't have heard him list any of those interests. Cousteau's first love wasn't with the blue seas of the ocean but rather with the blue skies above him. He joined the French navy when he was a young man, graduating from the naval academy in 1933 and being commissioned as a second lieutenant. His plan was to become a naval aviator.

His plan took a dramatic detour after a serious auto accident in northeastern France. Cousteau borrowed his father's Salmson sports car to attend a friend's wedding in the rolling hills near Bordeaux. Imagine the sort of racing car the Great Gatsby might have driven around. While navigating at night through the weaving roads in those hills, Cousteau lost control around a turn when the headlights went out. He would regain consciousness in the hospital after being saved by a random farm truck that just happened to drive by and spot him.

He had twelve broken bones, and his right arm was paralyzed. Cousteau refused the doctor's suggestion to have his infected arm amputated. While the infection would eventually go away and his fractures would heal, his flying days were over.

Some of us are born knowing we will never become a professional basketball player. But other times, the bright dreams we've spent years chasing and working toward might suddenly black out. We might suddenly veer off course from the road we've been heading down and find ourselves unable to go on. These very things can keep us stuck in place, or they can allow us to discover the very essence of who we are.

Cousteau would discover this during his rehab. He spent months of therapy swimming in order to help strengthen his broken bones. After a friend gave him a pair of swimming goggles, Cousteau would explore the ocean and come to see its beauty. These hours spent in the water opened up his mind and soul for something bigger—a life spent discovering more about it and allowing the rest of the world to see what he saw.

Fate is an interesting thing, isn't it? All the men in his class at the academy would end up being killed at the start of World War II several years later. Cousteau, however, would join the French Resistance movement during the war, becoming a spy who would eventually be nationally recognized and awarded several medals.

He was the James Bond of marine biology. How could you *not* fall in love with someone like Cousteau? And how could pursuing a career in this field not look enticing, especially for someone fascinated with the ocean and the world below it? One of the main reasons I chose to attend the University of Miami was because it had a great marine science program. There were other reasons I chose the University of Miami, of course. It was located in my home state of Florida, a very big plus for my family. I would receive a substantial scholarship from them as well. Many of my close friends from high school were headed there, too. But I was really interested in marine science, so it was a perfect fit.

My mother wasn't a fan of me trying to become a female Jacques Cousteau, however. There wasn't a lot of money in the field, so she worried about my ability to support myself. She would joke about me being eaten by a shark one day. And yes, I understood some of her reservations—especially since there was a very big problem, which I've already alluded to. I couldn't swim.

Due to my short stature, I had never truly learned how to swim with my head above water. I couldn't float; in fact, I sink. So dreams of diving into the deep and spending hours snorkeling and scuba diving were probably a bit like imagining myself becoming Supergirl and flying over the city. But I still thought I could probably do it.

I took classes in marine science in college, in pursuit of my dream. In one oceanography class, we took a field trip to the Florida Keys. While I was there, I realized the truth about my dreams. A simple exercise of surveying an area to count fish and plankton meant the instructor had to tie a rope around my waist to prevent me from drowning, since the floating thing was out of the question. It dawned on me during this field trip what the future looked like. I was never going to be the sort of ocean explorer I wanted to be.

If I pursued this field, I wouldn't be sailing on the seven seas and participating in deep-sea dives and uncovering great secrets of oceanography. I would be working in a lab studying the many facets of plankton. I would be missing out on discovering the universe undersea, and I would also be missing out on working and connecting with people. That wasn't going to work.

Of course, I realized in my classes that I absolutely hated physical chemistry, so that certainly helped with my grand epiphany. I had always been interested in studying medicine, and I switched my major to biology. While I was at it, I also received a degree in psychology, along with a minor in my much-maligned chemistry and marine biology. You know the rest of the story. I love medicine, and have found the profession that's right for me. It doesn't matter how realizations like this come to you—understanding when something isn't right for you affords you the opportunity to discover what is.

There's a quote I love from Jacques Cousteau: "Sometimes we are lucky enough to know that our lives have been changed, to discard the old, embrace the new, and run headlong down an immutable course."

Crashing that car in those French hills certainly did change the course of his life. Like Cousteau, I was forced to give up my dream—of becoming a marine biologist. But as he showed me, letting go of one dream can open the door to what you were really meant to do.

When life tells you "Absolutely not," I hope you will keep going. I hope you will be able to understand that that was not the right path, and that you will embrace the new and see where the course takes you.

DON'T LET THEM DEFINE YOU

Bill

I could hear the lyrics from that Violent Femmes song "Kiss Off" playing in my head. If there was ever a band that summed up and sounded how I felt at that moment, this alternative rock band popular in the eighties would be it.

This had been my—let's see—seventh in-person interview? I'd had more over the phone, but those always went great. On the opposite end of a phone receiver, I sounded like *the man*—confident and cocky and funny and easy to connect with. I was an alpha male, just like all salesmen had to be. Then, of course, as it always happened, the image of being a leader of a pack would suddenly evaporate the moment the interviewer took one glance down at me.

There was more than one meaning of the word "down" in this particular situation.

Instead of being an alpha dog strolling in, the interviewer would always appear to view me as some stray mutt. A mutt with a bit of a limp.

After spending five years of my life on crutches following my eighth-grade hip surgery, I was finally able to "walk" on my own during college. This had come after a lot of effort, frustration, and failure. My emancipation from crutches didn't mean I was a hundred percent healthy, however. I was only about two percent healthier than I needed to be to retire the crutches. My right and left hips were still dislocated and partially dislocated, respectively. Needless to say, my gait accentuated my already obvious "differences."

People always stopped noticing this soon after they got to know me, but it caused problems when I met with prospective employers after making the decision to go into pharmaceutical sales. They would call me in for an interview after reading my résumé, but when I showed up, I could see the reactions on their faces. They didn't have to articulate what they were thinking since their expressions read like subtitles in a movie.

He can't do the job.

We'll have to make special concessions for him.

How is this going to reflect on our business?

In a few of the interviews, it became clear the interviewer assumed my limitations were more substantial than they were in actuality. It almost felt like eventually they would ask me how long it was before I experienced spontaneous human combustion.

Speaking of combusting, this particular interview I was coming from had gone downhill the moment the interviewer saw me. Even though I hadn't said a word, I knew the woman had made her decision. It made me think of that *Seinfeld* episode where Kramer gets called into the boss's office only to be told his work stinks and there's no way they can possibly keep him on staff.

"I don't even really work here," Kramer said.

"That's what makes this so difficult," the boss replied.

This was so funny because Kramer in fact *didn't* have a job but rather had just started to show up in office meetings and began to keep going to them like a regular employee.

As I shared earlier in this book and also in our first book, getting a job after college was a frustrating process, to say the least. I've realized over the years that I would have been better served to switch my defensive mode of *how dare you act like that* to something a bit more like *okay fine here we go again, so let me help you.* It took me a while to figure out what exactly to say, but the obvious resistance and the rejection I experienced over and over caused me to decide I needed to try a different tactic. I decided that on the next interview, I was not leaving without addressing the elephant in the room.

This would prove to be a difficult thing to do. The psychology of the interview process is complex. Many times, my interviewer was thrown off by my mere presence. That turned into nervousness, which equated to being uncomfortable. And when they were uncomfortable, that meant their recollection of the interview was, to say the least, not optimal. In addition to this, employers can't make hiring decisions based on race, sex, or other characteristics or conditions. Since a lot of people aren't sure exactly what the rules are and whether they could ask about my limitations, we just never addressed it. So I wouldn't get a call back.

I was determined to address the situation on my next interview. I walked into the office, introduced myself, and shook the interviewer's hand with a confident smile.

"I'm sure you've noticed I am a bit shorter than average," I opened up by saying. "I'm not shy about my stature and I'd be more than happy to address any intelligent questions you might have, whether about my personal experiences or how I would perform at work."

The first time around, it didn't come out quite that polished. The second swing at bat, so to speak, was a lot better. The interviewer seemed relieved that I had released him from his prison cell of sticking to his script. I opened the door and he walked through it. We discussed some of the details of my medical past, and since I was trying to get a job, we also discussed how my stature would affect my job performance (not at all).

Opening up that door also opened up the possibility of them saying yes, but I didn't wind up getting that offer. In fact, while many of my subsequent interviews went more smoothly, they did not wind up being any more productive. As I've shared before, it would take around fifty interviews to finally receive an offer for a job.

People like to say "you can't take no for an answer." In my case, I couldn't let the no define who I was and what I was trying to do. So many of the no's had simply been based on the box people were putting me in. So I decided to keep the no's inside that box and step out of it.

Thankfully, I would eventually run into a manager who had stepped out of the box as well, one who would invite me to begin my professional career with them. And I have no doubt that you, too, will be able to find success if you take control, change the script, and don't take no for an answer.

DON'T LET THEM DISCOURAGE YOU

Jen

"Do you feel that someone of your stature will be able to adequately take care of your patients?"

The trauma surgeon sitting across from me was obviously playing the bad cop role, while the internal medicine doctor was the good cop. Five minutes into my interview to study at the University of Miami's Medical School, I felt like a doctor who had just come on call and suddenly had a patient going into an arrest. I couldn't stop and wonder why this was happening. I couldn't wait for my response. I just had to act.

"I understand I might not be the one to crack open the chest of a fifty-year-old man in a motor vehicle accident," I began to explain. "But there are many roles for physicians, and as someone who has grown up in and around hospitals, I'm very comfortable here. I understand my limitations and I would never put a patient in harm's way."

Initially, I was denied the opportunity to interview at my alma mater. I was as qualified as my peers who all received interviews, and I was suspicious that the inclusion of my stature in my personal essay as part of my application was to blame. When the president of the university, Dr. Foote, got wind of the fact that I hadn't been invited, he was shocked. Subsequent to our discussion, he made a phone call, and the following day I was offered an interview. I wish I could've told him it went great, but it didn't. With each question that came, it was obvious they were more concerned about my perceived *disabilities* than my abilities.

"So how do you drive a car?" the trauma surgeon asked.

I drove one here, so how about I show you? There I was, explaining something that had nothing to do with the interview.

"How are you going to get around the hospital?" the bad cop asked. "It's a really big place. We're spread out over a number of campuses."

I could only nod and smile. "That's a great question. I have a scooter, and I drive it around."

The internal medicine doctor, who was my cheerleader, said, "Yeah, I could see that, no problem."

"Well, how are you going to access the patient?" the trauma surgeon asked.

"I have a step stool," I said. "I imagine I could bungee cord it to my scooter and I'd see my patients that way."

I knew the world of medicine was full of gifted doctors, some of whom were very full of themselves. This surgeon's philosophy as we spoke came through loud and clear. It was his belief that anybody entering the field of medicine should be physically and mentally capable of working in any and all of the specialties and subspecialties a doctor is afforded to pursue, rather than to focus on the one that is most interesting to the individual.

With each subsequent question the surgeon asked me, and with each passing shade of red deepening on my face, I attempted to answer each question the best way I could. I stood my ground and became reminded of one of the many reasons why I felt like I could excel in this field: *Knowing how to care for people isn't enough. You have to care about them.*

The dismissive air and arrogance on the man's face weren't the only infuriating things that were occurring. He had actually gotten me to doubt my desire about getting into medicine in the first place.

The smiling face of the poster hanging in my room when I was a girl came to mind. Some girls had grown up having posters of rock star bad boys or hunky movie actors in their rooms. I had a picture of a teenage doctor named Doogie Howser. Surely you've heard of him, right? *Doogie Howser, M.D.,* was one of my favorite shows growing up. How could I not love a show about a young genius who would become a sixteen-year-old surgeon? Especially when that show starred a young Neil Patrick Harris?

During this barrage of doubt from the trauma surgeon interviewing me, I couldn't help thinking of one of my favorite moments on *Doogie Howser, M.D.* It was when a patient realized how young the teenage doctor was.

"Wait a minute. You're a kid," the patient said.

Doogie Howser didn't back down, but rather replied with a classic line.

"True, but I'm also a genius. If you have a problem with that, I can get you an older doctor who's not as smart as me."

I felt like telling these men, "Sure, I'm short. But I'm also the brightest and most personable candidate you're going to find. If you have a problem, I can find you a taller applicant."

It wouldn't be hard finding a taller applicant. But it would be hard for them to find someone more interested in improving the health of others.

I refused to let this interview discourage me. And two weeks later, I took my pride and my confidence with me to interview with the people at Johns Hopkins School of Medicine. It would be the only other interview I'd receive, but this one would be completely different. I met with a pediatrician, and he sat down with me and actually asked me many questions.

"Jennifer, why do you want to become a doctor?" the pediatrician asked.

So I shared the many reasons why I wanted to become one. I shared my journey, from wanting to be a marine biologist to why I felt a desire to enter the medical field. I shared about Dr. Kopits and about growing up in hospitals. The man asked me about my extracurricular activities and what kind of field I wanted to go into. He was talking about everything and anything unrelated to my stature. At one point during the interview, I had a strange thought come over me.

Does he actually know I'm a Little Person?

This had been such a different experience from my other interview. He had never addressed my stature once. I knew I needed to address it. The pediatrician either had no problem with me being a Little Person or he was afraid to talk about it. Either things were going really, really well or really, really badly. I had to say something.

"You know, I'll probably need a step stool to see patients."

He only gave me a nod. "Okay, no problem."

"And you know—I'll probably need a scooter to get around campus."

"Certainly. That would be no problem. Is there anything else you think you'll need?"

"No, I don't think so," I said. "I won't really know until I get here, but that would probably be the most of it."

"Okay—great," he said.

He's genuinely interested in me and wants to know how he can help.

Soon he was showing me pictures of his kids and wishing me well before I got a tour of the hospital. On the tour, I had a chance to visit the dome. It was in that place where the term "rounds" was created. Talk about inspiration.

It sure felt like the University of Miami was giving me a big NO. That experience could have stamped a permanent rejection seal over any future attempts to go to medical school. Yet I had continued on, and had a fabulous second interview.

Surprisingly enough, about two weeks later, I actually got a call from the University of Miami and got offered a seat in the School of Medicine's class of 2000. And then I also got a call from the dean of admissions at Johns Hopkins, and I got offered a seat there for the class of 2000. So I was very blessed that I had two options.

You can guess which school I decided to say "yes" to. It was the one that actually had faith in me, regardless of my stature. It also happened to be my dream school. I very happily graduated from Johns Hopkins after four of the roughest years of my life.

You can't listen to no's and the negativity that's out there. You can't let someone else's limited vision suddenly begin to narrow your own. Even when you hear someone say you can't, you have to continue to know the things that are possible. You have to believe the things you know you're capable of.

I knew I couldn't become a trauma surgeon, but I did know that I could become a pediatrician or a geneticist or an ophthalmologist or *something* in the field of medicine that would allow me to care for patients.

Soon, we're going to talk more about the ideas of Knowing something and Believing in something. But those two things will always require you to have to reject no's that can come your way. Don't be afraid to believe in yourself, even when no one else believes in you.

TURN YOUR "NO" INTO A "NOW WHAT?"

Bill and Jen

We live in an interesting culture, where people seem to celebrate no's just as much as any sort of yes. For instance, remember when *American Idol* began to air? It was more compelling to see the singers who were rejected than it was to see those who actually made it through to compete on the show, especially when you had a judge like Simon Cowell giving input to the singers. You waited to hear what sort of comments he would come up with, and took joy in hearing him beat down the singers who should never have auditioned in the first place.

Can you imagine going in front of judges, with cameras aimed at you and a whole crew watching you in the background, and then singing? And then receiving comments like this one:

"It was absolutely terrible in most parts. I mean, it was like being at a funeral for the first half."

Ouch. Surely Simon must have been in a bad mood to say such a brutal thing to a contestant, right? But oh, no. He came up with quite the list of rejections, like the following creative one:

"That song was like going to a zoo or something. I mean, the noises were beyond anything I have ever, ever heard."

It wasn't just a simple "No thanks." America has grown used to watching people win in spectacular fashion and people being rejected in the same way.

But you don't have to look far to see that some of the most successful people out there are ones who have heard "no" numerous times.

Take, for instance, the actor who got a note from a casting director after his first screen test that said, "Can't act. Slightly bald. But can dance a little."

Well, good thing the actor had a *little* potential. Turns out Fred Astaire would become known as one of the greatest dancers of all time and would become the star of many musical comedies.

Think of all the authors who had their famous manuscripts rejected. One of the most famous is J. K. Rowling, who had *Harry Potter and the Sorcerer's Stone* turned down a dozen times. And even after a publisher decided to publish it, her editor told her not to quit her day job. Such confidence for a project that would eventually become the bestselling book series of all time.

A singer who was just starting out once performed at the Ryman Auditorium in Nashville while on the Grand Ole Opry radio program. The manager of the show told the singer something Simon Cowell might have said himself:

"You ain't going nowhere, son. You ought to go back to driving a truck."

This son going nowhere happened to be Elvis Presley. He didn't go back to driving a truck but rather ended up becoming known as the King of Rock & Roll and one of the bestselling artists of all time.

You could write a book called *The Book of No's* about all the greats who were rejected at one point (or many points) in their life. Walt Disney was famously told he lacked an imagination. Michael Jordan was cut by his high school basketball team. Steve Jobs was fired by Apple, the company he had created. Albert Einstein was expelled from high school for his poor work and failed a college entrance exam. Even the great Abraham Lincoln is known for all the failures he overcame, including being defeated when running for U.S. Congress and U.S. Senate and even for vice president.

These people, who were all told no, went on to tell the world *yes*.

Everybody is told no sometimes. There might be some in this world who end up hearing it more often for whatever reason, but the number of no's you hear doesn't mean you should give up.

Perhaps it simply means you're stepping out and trying more than most people.

Maybe it means you knocked on a door that needed to stay closed, leaving you free to find success elsewhere.

Maybe it's a chance for you to figure out a different way to tell your story.

When you Think Big, the word "no" should actually sound more like "now what?"

HOW TO SHAKE OFF THE NO'S OF LIFE

1. Whenever someone says you can't do something, write their statement on a note card and keep it in your desk. Pull it out when you've shown that you can. Don't worry about proving *them* wrong. Prove to yourself you're right.

2. Do you have a bulletin board hanging up somewhere? No? Then buy one today and put it up in your house or office or basement or garage. Stick a picture (or several) on it of something you can't have or do. If it's some *no* in your life that you feel could one day be a *yes*, then put it up there so you can visualize it. If it's that Audi A8 that you can see in your dreams, then put it on the board. If it's children, put some family photos on there. Perhaps it's just hope for the future. Put an inspiring quote or a Bible verse on the board.

3. Remember the iconic training scene from the original *Rocky*? If you've never seen it, Google it, like, *now*. We're not suggesting you go don some sweats and a cap and

start running around your neighborhood. But when you've been pushed and put into a corner, whether in your career or your personal life, get yourself psyched up. Find some sort of inspiration, whether it's physical or emotional. Take a long drive or a bike ride. Find a body of water—a lake or pond or river or ocean—and simply stand by it for a while. Go have a beer or a glass of wine with a friend. Read a motivational book (oh, wait, you're already doing that). Do something, anything that will light any sort of spark inside of you.

4. Ask for help. Your spouse and family and friends are in your life for this. When you have some sort of struggle or setback, share it with others. Maybe you just need someone to be a sounding board. Or maybe you really do need professional or personal advice. Lean on your loved ones. Even your children, regardless of their ages. There's a lot of wisdom and truth in a four- and a five-year-old. The world hasn't beaten them down yet, so they still don't realize all the no's they'll encounter in life. Soak up any advice or encouragement or affection you can. Lord knows we all need it.

5. Laugh. Find some way—any way—to make fun of yourself and to chuckle at the world. Go on YouTube to find funny videos. Text your friends or family members nonsense. Go somewhere to play, whether it's a sport or simply playing with your kids on a playground. Pour a

little fun into your life and remind yourself the point is about living and giving back. A no is just a speed bump in a parking lot. That doesn't mean you can't drive a sports car and get your motor runnin' and head out on the highway . . . Adventure will come your way as long as you get past those no's.

CHAPTER FIVE

KNOW

*"Know yourself. Don't accept your dog's admiration
as conclusive evidence that you are wonderful."*

—Ann Landers

ACCEPT CERTAINTIES

Jen

We have learned over the years. I'm adept in the medical specialty
of taking care of babies who are newborn, sick, or premature, a
field known as neonatology. Bill is skillful at starting businesses
and organizing people and processes to run a creative enterprise, a
role known as an entrepreneur. Of course, we know a thing or two
about skeletal dysplasia and surgeries. We understand the world of
Little People in big ways. And we know a little about littler Little
People, a.k.a. our children. We also know something about dogs,

currently having two of them living with us as we write this book. Some things we know a little bit about and other things we know a lot about.

There are other things Bill and I know for a fact: The truth of Bill's obsession with cars. The certainty of my love of fashion. And the reality that neither of us will ever play professional basketball.

Sooner or later, all of us have to know our capabilities and limitations. These are what you might call the facts of life, and they're something you come to accept more with each passing birthday. It's one thing to grow up as a child with hopes and dreams. Those hopes are blessings you have inside of you, to hold on to for as long as you can. As I've mentioned earlier in this book, I held on to the belief for a while that one day I'd wake up as a tall person. I truly believed this for a period of time in my life. I believe that growing older and gaining wisdom isn't just about acquiring life experience, it's also about accepting what we can and can't do. Because truly, none of us are able to do everything and anything.

I played some baseball when I was a kid. Yet clearly I wasn't going to become a pro sports player. It's probably out of my realm of capabilities, at least for most sports. Maybe I could have tried table tennis or something. But that's okay, because there are a lot of good things that I could do, despite my disability and stature. The important thing about succeeding in life and achieving our dreams is truly knowing your capabilities.

Every now and then, however, someone will come along and seemingly exceed those expectations and capabilities. Our dog Maggie is one of those crazy exceptions.

Here's another truth Bill and I would have shared before we got our pets: Dogs can't fly. Yet nobody bothered to tell Maggie this.

Talking about things people know, it's no big revelation to say Bill and I love our dogs. Anyone who has ever seen our show can see this. Anybody who owns a pet store named after their two dogs certainly has to be an animal lover. Rocky and Maggie were our first children and our training ground for parenting.

We like to say that our Chihuahua, Rocky, is basically an old man. If you've ever been around a Chihuahua, Rocky is the absolute opposite of their typical personality. Even though the breed can be all over the map, the perception of Chihuahuas tends to be that they're feisty and will bark at anything and everything. Seven-pound Rocky is a snuggler who will go to anything that generates heat. This includes wandering over to our oven after we've been cooking and lying down beside it. Bill likes to say we're going to put some barbecue sauce on him one day. He's always searching for the warmest spot in the house, whether it's in a spot of sun in the kitchen or in his familiar position next to me on the bed. Both of us sleep with our heads in the same direction on the pillow. Sometimes it sort of freaks Bill out a bit.

If Rocky is an old man, then Maggie is our rambunctious toddler. The seven-pound terrier mix is our rescue mutt who seems to show her appreciation for being saved every second of every day. She's overly excited about everything. She will jump all over Rocky and do the same to you when you sit down on the couch. One moment she'll be trying to lick your ear, then you'll go to move her and she'll be bouncing around in your lap. Rocky is like the big brother too cool to be bothered, while Maggie is the baby sister who is always hanging on to his every move.

Here's another fact about Maggie: Not only is she as active and moves as much as a hummingbird, but she also thinks she can fly. We learned this one morning while Bill was at home working. He told me the wild story when I got home that night.

When we built our dream house, we worked with a builder and architect to customize the home in every way we could. Since we were in our thirties, Bill and I knew and had accepted our limitations. So we went into designing the house with that in mind, eliminating a lot of those limitations. For instance, we'd spent our whole lives having to climb on stools and using grabbers simply to reach for simple items on counters. This was our chance to make life easier for ourselves and design a house with low counters and cabinets.

With my job demanding a lot of my time and energy, I relied on Bill to make some of the creative choices. Kitchen counters and cupboards were lowered, along with the stovetop and sink. These made it easier for us to cook and clean up. Yet some things remained standard, like the dining island in the kitchen. This was so we could accommodate guests while we were entertaining. Some decisions were compromises, such as one bathroom downstairs at an average height for guests and another designed for us. Even our windows were a lower height than usual since we would be the ones primarily looking out of them.

One choice we made when we built the house wasn't exactly thought through completely when it came to having children. Bill's office is in an open area upstairs, overlooking our living room. When it was just Bill and me and the two dogs, he could work there in peace and quiet. With the arrival of Will and Zoey, the volume level went up quite a bit, and it's a bit harder to concentrate there. There is a door to an outdoor balcony on one side where you can walk out and look out over the backyard.

Bill had been working that morning with Maggie sleeping in the dog bed next to his desk. He explained to me later he was talking on the phone and decided to step outside onto the balcony for some fresh air, leaving the door open. As he spoke to the client, he saw something out of the corner of his eye inside the house.

Maggie was launching herself from the ledge above the living room onto the first floor. Bill only saw a fluffy blur of motion, which he thought he had surely imagined.

He quickly got off the phone and ran back inside, positive his eyes and mind were playing tricks on him. He stared at his chair next to the built-in cabinets, then looked at the dog bed, where Rocky lay with an expression on his face as if to say, "Yup, she jumped." Bill called out for Maggie but couldn't find her. He quickly peered over the fifteen-foot drop, still not believing the dog would do something like that, then ran down the stairs.

"I swear, I thought I was going to find her on the ground as dead as a doornail," Bill told me.

But Maggie stood on the bottom step wagging her tail. She actually looked like she was ready to do it again. Bill couldn't believe it, and neither could I after he told me.

"I'm pretty sure I figured out *how* she did it," he said. "I think she jumped up onto my chair, then jumped onto the shelves and wandered over to the ledge, and then jumped."

That wasn't the part neither of us could understand. We couldn't figure out how in the world she survived her jump.

"Does she not know she's a dog?" I joked with Bill. "Doesn't she realize she can't fly?"

"I honestly don't know," Bill said.

While it's nice to resist the no's that can be put into your life, and while it's great to try things out, it's also nice to have common sense. We're not sure whether Maggie did eventually learn she couldn't fly. We did, however, make sure to prevent it from ever happening again. Bill knows better now than to leave his empty chair near the shelves for Maggie to jump on.

The point: Well, Maggie survived her jump, but we really like our dog, and think she should not attempt it again. She cannot fly, whether she understands that or not. She has the limitation of being a dog, just as Bill and I have limitations because of our dysplasia. Everyone has limitations, and it's important to understand and accept those. Maggie is not a bird. I will never play in the NBA.

What limitations do you have that are hard to accept? The first step is knowing what those limitations are.

MAKE ADJUSTMENTS

- -

Bill

I have endured more than twenty-five surgeries in my lifetime. One of my first memories is of waking up in the operating room at Johns Hopkins Hospital when I was three years old. I remember the bright lights hovering above me, the chatter in the background, and the awful, antiseptic smell that has been burned into my olfactory memory forever.

While that first surgery wound up working out pretty well, not all of my surgeries resulted in the planned goal. In fact, when I was in the tenth grade, I had one surgery that went pretty badly.

Let's be honest—being fifteen years old can be pretty tough to begin with. Pimples are a given, and chances are you're in the midst of going through puberty, and your body is continuing to change on a daily basis. For boys, your pituitary gland is producing hormones leading to the release of testosterone, which wreaks havoc on your every sense. Hair is sprouting everywhere; your voice is continuing its debate over which octave to settle on. Things are growing rapidly, and some things grow at rather inappropriate times . . . Well, like I said, your body is changing a lot; girls are becoming the most wonderful and terrifying creatures you can ever imagine. So adding a major surgery to this mix was a real bummer.

I had grown used to walking around on crutches for several years. This was a result of a surgery in seventh grade, and I hoped to wean myself off crutches after rehabilitation. For a while I could actually walk around without aids and began to see some progress.

One morning, after a day of working at a campground store helping people and carrying items with no problem, I woke up unable to walk. It turned out one of my hip joints had filled with synovial fluid. This fluid basically helps cushion your hip. In fact, so much synovial fluid had built up and inflamed the area that my hip had been literally pushed out of its socket.

I just planned to grin and bear it and get through the pain. Of course, I had no plan on how I'd actually be able to walk again. Mom had other plans, bringing me to Dr. Kopits's office for an exam. He admitted me to the hospital and a day later I was being wheeled into radiology to get something called an arthrogram. This is where they stick six-to-eight-inch-long needles in your legs in order to fill the space around your joints with dye to show the contrast between the bones and soft tissues. The dye has to be in place for the doctor to know where the problems are. One of my big problems was the synovial fluid had to be removed. Dr. Kopits was able to remove nearly three cups of it before the end of that day.

The problem with this procedure was I hadn't been put under for it. So to say I was screaming in pain really doesn't do it justice. The following day, when they did more tests, I'd be put under.

Even after that procedure, my hip never did get better. The femoral head wouldn't reseat into the socket properly. The result was that for the following two years I'd be on crutches. After two years of failed rehabilitation, I was still using crutches to get around, and I had no choice but to go under the knife again in tenth grade.

My mother and I traveled to Baltimore, Maryland, for the procedure. Thanksgiving had just passed and we hoped I could be discharged in time to be home for Christmas. My longtime physician, Dr. Kopits, was training a successor, Dr. Afiche. Together, they conceived of a plan in which they would repair both of my hips. Dr. Kopits performed the surgery on the right hip, the worse of the two since it was completely dislocated; Dr. Afiche performed the surgery on the partially dislocated left.

The first surgery, which took place on December 9, proved difficult. I woke up nearly twenty-four hours after I had gone into the operating room. When I was coherent enough to talk, I was greeted by Dr. Kopits.

"Billy, my friend."

Right there, I knew I was in trouble. His thick Hungarian accent was a warm blanket when he wanted to calm your nerves, but the inflection in his voice always told the truth.

"I did my best to save the hip," he said. "I was able to reshape the femoral head and reseat it within the reshaped acetabulum. But the bone is simply too malleable. I knew before we closed you up that the hip will soon dislocate again."

There was an uncomfortable pause. I was now clued into what everyone else in the room, including my doctor and parents, had known for almost a day. Here come the quotes from *The Godfather* . . . "My wife is crying upstairs. I hear cars coming to the house. Consigliore of mine, I think it's time you told your Don what everyone seems to know," said Don Corleone to Tom Hagen. The surgery had been unsuccessful and I would likely need crutches to walk for the foreseeable future.

This makes me think of another famous line from the movie *The Godfather Part III*, released a year after this surgery:

"Just when I thought I was out . . . they pull me back in."

Michael Corleone dreaded going back to the life of crime he had tried to escape. I suddenly loathed the idea of moving around in life with crutch #1 and crutch #2 underneath my arms again.

Incidentally, that was one of the only good lines in *The Godfather III*. However, *The Godfather* and *The Godfather II* were nothing short of awesome. "A kid comes up to me in a white jacket, gives me a Ritz cracker and chopped liver, he says, 'Canapes,' I say, 'Can o' peas my a$*! That's a Ritz cracker and chopped liver,'" said Pentangeli. I could do this all day, but I might need Puzo and Coppola to sign off on it if I quote any more . . . But I digress.

Back to the story . . . To make matters worse, I spiked a fever that evening. An infection had developed at the surgical site. Dr. Kopits opened the cast the next day, cutting a window around the wound so it could be cleaned up and redressed. Thankfully, the infection was quickly thwarted and I was cleared for the left hip to be reconstructed the following week.

Ten days later, I was back under the knife. The good news was I still had my IV, so things like blood work and a new IV placement weren't necessary. That was the only silver lining I could see in this situation, but after the week I'd had, it felt like a shining example of positivity.

Surgery was, once again, arduous. The left hip proved to be as complicated a procedure as the right. After nearly twelve hours of surgery, I was wheeled into the recovery room with all of the other miserable patients recovering from their surgeries. Fun fact: Misery does not love company. All I wanted was to be alone.

When I was finally moved to my room the following morning, I again met with the doctors. Both Kopits and Afiche came to visit me this time around. They got down to business pretty quickly.

"The left hip fared better than the right, but we saw much of the same disease state in the left hip as we did on the right side," Dr. Kopits said. "Therefore, while there is a chance this reconstruction effort will 'take,' it is also unlikely it will give you many years before it will need to be replaced."

I couldn't believe it. Twelve days after being admitted, I had gone through two procedures, both of which had failed. Even worse, I was facing another twelve weeks wrapped up in a body cast while my unsuccessfully repaired hips and surrounding tissue healed. It was not exactly the Christmas gift I'd been hoping for.

The silver lining was that I was able to return home to New York before the holiday. All my friends were as disappointed as I was with the bad news. I had hoped and planned to be healing up, enjoying the holiday, having fun and being optimistic about the prospect of being "crutch-free" when I emerged from the cast in a few months.

For a while I still had hope that I'd put these surgeries behind me and would eventually walk and run like anybody else. I still had a mind-set of hope, along with the fire of refusing to give up and trying to eventually tell those crutches "No more." Yet I would have to learn a lesson in understanding limitations. And some lessons sting.

In the spring I headed back to Baltimore to have my cast removed and begin physical therapy. My parents stayed with me for about a week before they returned to New York to go back to work. I spent the following two months in the hospital—for the most part alone. I was assigned Room 313, a quiet single room stuffed away in the corner. I appreciated the solitude, as I was focused on getting better and getting out of the hospital. And "13" was my lucky number . . . so I had that going for me, which is nice.

I had physical therapy twice a day, once in the morning, and once in the afternoon. After a couple of weeks, a routine emerged. Breakfast at 8:00 a.m., exercises and stretching in the morning, a BLT and iced tea for lunch. In the afternoon, most of my exercises were done in the pool. Dinner was rather unremarkable, though I was bingeing on lemon meringue pie, which was, for some reason, unexpectedly tasty. My teachers had sent along schoolwork to local tutors who came to the hospital. I could keep up with my class during my free time, and it kept my mind active.

By the tenth week it became apparent that I had reached the limit of what I would accomplish during inpatient therapy. I was walking on crutches and able to navigate stairs, which meant I was eligible for discharge. In these ten weeks, something inside of me began to change. It wasn't the solitary confinement of my situation, nor was it the hard work of rehab. The reality of waking up and going to bed in the hospital reinforced a truth I'd been walking around with my whole life.

I knew I had skeletal dysplasia, but now I knew something else. *I have limitations. Quite a few, in fact.*

When I arrived home, I reintegrated into my tenth-grade class just in time for finals, Regents exams (standardized tests in New York), and the summer. I finished the grade on crutches. While the surgical procedures were seen as failures, the experience as a whole was a turning point in my life.

In the previous chapters, we spoke about roadblocks and obstacles in people's lives. So many pioneers, experts, and other successful people say that they would not be where they are today if they had not experienced some kind of hurdle or failure in their past. We also shared about experiences where we had been told no or denied something, yet had moved on from there.

This, however, was different. This had been no failure of my own. This had simply been life up to this point for me, and I suddenly understood how it would inform my future.

Being laid up in a body cast and isolated in a hospital with only my books to keep me occupied was great for my GPA. I made the honor roll and aced all of my final exams. Ending the year strong from an academic standpoint allowed me to enter the summer with a different mind-set. With the chance to reflect over the summer, I began to appreciate my limitations. Moreover, I began to adjust to accommodate my limitations instead of ignore them.

I couldn't rely on my body, at least not the way I'd been doing up to that point. I knew I wasn't going to rebound the way we all hoped after the surgery. There were going to be lots of things in life I couldn't do, especially from a physical standpoint. I needed to take things easy in certain areas. I also realized that if I wanted to get anywhere in life, I was going to need to have a good head on my shoulders. I was going to have to continue taking my studies seriously, and I was going to have to focus on proving myself academically. And I'd have to get a car.

This was going to be hard work. It wasn't going to be simple, like flipping a switch to turn it on, but then, anything worth doing isn't. Once I acknowledged my very real limitations, I knew that I needed to change my habits, focus, and start heading down a new road—crutches and all. It turned out to be the very best thing I could have done.

LIMITATIONS CAN LIBERATE

Jen

When you're a child, you can't wait to become an adult and be able to do anything you want. Yet the older you become, you come to realize you're just not as young and energetic as you used to be. A man can look in the mirror and remember that full head of hair he used to have. Or the deep brown color that's been replaced by gray. A woman might remember the years she spent excited to see her body filling out, but now she's wishing she could fit into those slender jeans she used to be able to wear.

We all know that if we're lucky, we'll be senior citizens one day. We also know something the late Steve Jobs summed up in an eloquent way: "Death is the destination we all share. No one has ever escaped it."

In some ways, however, I feel like I did dodge it, at least temporarily, after being diagnosed with stage three choriocarcinoma that began with the molar pregnancy. It was yet another uphill battle and a difficult struggle, but it was quite a thrill to be able to tweet my victory to the rest of the world on January 16, 2015:

One year cancer free TODAY! #Celebrate!

Yet even before my health scare, while we were in India finally meeting Zoey and taking her home, I had started to have this realization that I needed to scale back in life. With the adjustment of having Will in our lives, I began to see life in a whole new way. I wouldn't say I was staring downhill preparing to coast in a convertible, with Bill driving. Nobody coasts when it comes to having one child under the age of five, much less two of them.

Even all the way back to medical school, I knew there would be some physically demanding realities of my job, especially considering my stature. Being on your feet all day is one thing. And yes, I have the benefit of being able to drive a scooter around for long distances. But a lot of doctors and nurses are able to sit on chairs during the day. For me, a workstation task chair still comes up to my nose, so I have to use a step stool to sit down, something I'm not going to do repeatedly. I'd rather just stand. Every time I see a patient, I'll go up and down on the step stool, so every day for me is a StairMaster workout.

The reality, even before kids and cancer, was that my body wouldn't allow me to retire from my job at eighty years of age. Growing up, my parents advised me to use my brain, not my body, to find a rewarding and self-supporting career. So, like Bill learned during those high school years after hip surgery, I knew I needed to focus on academic work. With my love of medical education and my involvement with the simulation center, it only seemed natural to begin to scale back on seeing patients.

Bill had the realization that he needed to focus more on his studies and to rely on his head to get him places. I had already spent years doing this, but suddenly after battling cancer, I gained a different perspective.

Life is short.

And no, that's not just a plug for the first book we wrote (but you can find it wherever books are sold!). I had a whole new appreciation for just how short life could really be. I could have lost mine, and I came out of my cancer battle with a question: *Why am I killing myself staying so busy and exhausted?*

Back when I was young and in school and residency, I could work long hours and didn't have as many responsibilities as I do now. When Bill came along, he actually helped with some of the responsibilities in my life. He was someone I could lean on (and still do all the time!). But I was, as the saying goes, no spring chicken. I felt more like it was the end of summer and I needed to start figuring out how I was going to spend my fall.

With the tsunami of cancer and Bill's back surgery arriving just as our family went from two to four, I knew scaling back was a must. The cancer wasn't the only way my body was telling me to take it easy. I had a neck issue that developed, and I couldn't escape the fact that I spent a lot of time looking up or down at patients as part of my job. I had to bend my neck back and forth all throughout the day.

There would be evenings when I would come home and be too physically exhausted to do much of anything, let alone chase two kids around until bedtime. When Bill was incapacitated and recovering from surgery, it was a good reminder of how I wanted and needed to do more with Will and Zoey. I knew I didn't want to quit the job I loved so much. Yet I realized I also wanted to be able to enjoy being a mom.

We all learn our limitations eventually, whether we easily accept them or wage a fierce boxing match against them. Accepting those limitations doesn't mean we give up our hopes and dreams, it may just mean we reevaluate or modify them. When I was in the midst of my battle with cancer, I wasn't waving a white flag and settling in. I was digging in my trench, keeping my head down to avoid the gunfire and bomb blasts.

I hope to one day be twice my current age, having been able to see what life looks like on the other side of the mountain. I expect it to be more beautiful and more fulfilling. I hope to be able to sit on a porch holding Bill's hand and reciting the lines of the famous Dylan Thomas as my personal motto: "Do not go gentle into that good night . . . Rage, rage against the dying of the light."

We can't do anything about that dying of the light. Yet we can try to allow it to burn bright as long as there is a flame. Remember, a candle can be all shapes and sizes. That doesn't impact how intense the wick can burn.

Accepting my limitations now means I'll hopefully keep burning for much longer.

KNOW THE DIFFERENCE BETWEEN
CONFIDENCE AND CAUTION

Bill

Life can feel like one constant set of warnings following you every-where you go: a winter storm watch or a severe thunderstorm warn-ing. Toy safety information and nutritional facts labels. Warning signs of a heart attack. A fuel light popping on indicating you're low on gas. A beach warning flag. A road-closed sign. The 250 different things you need to do to set up a child's car seat. That look of quea-siness from your child that tells you *look out*.

Some warnings seem like pranks pulled by members of a fra-ternity house. For instance, for us men out there, have you ever wondered why they have to put up signs in public restrooms that say "Please do not eat the urinal cakes"? Is there any human being out there who would really grab one of those light blue or whitish-colored deodorizer blocks resembling a hockey puck out of a *public urinal*? Maybe calling it names like cakes, mints, biscuits, cook-ies, or donuts makes guys hungry. As Melman says in *Madagascar*, "Look! Free mints!"

Sometimes warnings make it seem like an editor didn't catch the obvious. Like the warning on *children's* cough medicine saying "Do not drive car or operate machinery." Yes, I always have to re-mind Will not to take his convertible out for a ride after I give him a dose of children's cough medicine. Clearly, I am dating myself as I have learned that that type of good old-fashioned cough syrup is no longer prescribed for children. Speaking of machinery, it's a good thing they warn us before using a chain saw by saying "Do not hold the wrong end of a chain saw." Or the Huebsch commercial washing machine that says "DO NOT put any person in this washer." Oh, that's right . . . we have to take our clothes off before we wash them.

The world is so full of warnings that it can be easy to start to take them for granted. Especially when they have something to do with ourselves.

After my surgery at fifteen and the time recovering on crutches, I knew my body had quite a few limitations set on it. If the term "twerking" had been coined back then, they would have had a warning sign with my picture attached next to it. Yes, certain types of dance moves involving the hips were out of the question. But that didn't mean I needed to give up on the rest of my body.

The "special" phys ed program at my high school was run by Mr. Musso, a former weight lifter and all-around nice guy. For the remainder of my time in high school, I had PE just like every other student, but my gym class consisted of lifting weights and playing badminton. Because of my hips, I had never been a runner, so I was always a spectator for most team sports. But it turned out that I was a surprisingly great weight lifter. I never would have tried weight lifting if it hadn't been for those failed surgeries, but my unfortunate circumstances unveiled a hidden talent I would enjoy for many years. Because of my limitations, I discovered talents I didn't know I had.

It's one thing to nurture those talents. It's another thing to push ourselves beyond our limits.

This is where being overzealous can come to bite us in our bottoms. Or in my case, in the spine.

Fast-forward to about four years ago, around 2012. It was the start of a new year and I had decided to get back into shape, so I was going to the gym to work out with a personal trainer. He knew about my situation and had even spoken to the doctor who performed my hip replacement surgeries to better understand my limitations. I began lifting with him on and off, trying new things in order to generate strength. It felt like old times. I felt like the old Bill Klein.

My personal trainer had told me to be careful. But he and I also wanted to make progress. So we scanned the gym and found the kettle bells sitting in the corner with no one in line to use them. So we went over, picked out a reasonably weighted kettle bell, and went through the motions of the exercise. It was only a ten-pound kettle bell, so lifting it wasn't going to be a problem. The instruction was to lift with your knees and not your back. But that's easy to say and not so easy to do when you're a Little Person and you've basically always lifted with your back. I tried to lift with my knees, but happened to also lift with my back. And with my first thrust upward . . . I felt a pinch in my back.

That's not good.

I realized that perhaps we didn't need to diversify my exercise routine as much as I had originally aspired to do. My back was sore, but I kept working out for the next two weeks, assuming it was going to get better. Eventually I had to stop working out altogether. In the weeks that followed, the sharp, shooting pain I was experiencing continued to persist and even intensify. My trainer suggested we take a break, which was necessary since the slightest thing—like just tripping on an uneven sidewalk—would feel like someone was zapping my back with a cattle prod.

I began to fear the worst. I knew my body and knew I had injured myself badly. Very badly. I soon found out it would require surgery. Of course, I knew a few other things, too. We were planning on adopting Will, and then once we made plans to travel and bring him back home, we also learned we would be bringing Zoey home in the months that followed Will's arrival. Since I didn't want there to be any delays imposed on getting our kids, I put off having the surgery. So when we went to get Will, the pain continued. Then we got Zoey and the pain continued to rage like some wildfire. Then Jen got diagnosed, so of course I wasn't about to have any sort of dramatic surgery then.

I had, in fact, gone to see a local surgeon after we had brought Will back home. The surgeon had said we could try this and try that, but I just shook my head and refused to have any more of these sorts of conversations.

"We're not going to *try* anything," I told him.

The surgeon had very little experience with my type of skeletal dysplasia, and as Dr. Kopits knew too well, people like Jen and me are unique to operate on. For most surgeons, we might as well have alien anatomy. There was no way I was going to let someone simply "try" a surgery on me.

I eventually sent my info to a special hip doctor. No, not a doctor who works on hips, but a hip and cool doctor who also happens to specialize in caring for people with complex spinal issues. So after nine months of dialogue and going back and forth I eventually saw him. After the examination, he couldn't believe what he was seeing.

"You have a vertebral disc in your back that's herniated," the doctor told me. "I'm surprised you're not in more pain."

Basically I had a disc stuck in my spinal cord. It wasn't pretty and it sure was painful. For someone like me with short stature, this was definitely not the best news. Our vertebrae are different—many things are different inside of our bodies. So I couldn't continue to put off repairing this injury any longer.

Yet life happens, and there's nothing you can do about it. It's like passing a sign that says winding roads are ahead. The sign doesn't mean you shouldn't keep driving. But every now and then when you are going around those curves of life, you'll blow out a tire.

I had the occasion to think about a conversation I had with a friend right before I hurt my back. I had met Bobby Van Etten when I was just a kid. He's short in stature and older than me, and while I was in the hospital being treated by Dr. Kopits, Bobby allowed me to stay with him in Baltimore. He mentored younger kids like me by being an example of what's possible if you apply yourself in school and don't listen to the "no's." He had already graduated college and was an engineer. I remember him letting me drive for the first time in my life—being a Little Person meant Bobby's car was set up with controls that fit me almost as well at the ripe old age of ten. I also remember going to the movies to see *Star Trek 3: The Search for Spock* with him. We've stayed in touch over the past thirty years and Bobby and his wonderful wife, Angela, came to our wedding in 2008.

ABOVE: Bill pumping iron with his first barbell, circa 1981.

ABOVE: Jen dressed as Tinkerbell.

LEFT: Bill and his brother Tom being tied up by their uncle Patrick (approximately 1981).

RIGHT: Jen and her younger brother, David, practicing a little baseball by the side of their house.

LEFT: Bill and his brothers, Tom and Joe, and stepbrothers, Jonathan and James.

RIGHT: Jen on the merry-go-round at the World's Fair. Notice the men's belt holding her cast in place. Her dad was just to the left of the photo.

LEFT: Bill in his New York Giants gear . . . at his mom's house.

LEFT: Dr. Kopits in his office.

RIGHT: Jen and Dr. Foote at graduation from the University of Miami in 1996.

LEFT: Jen and Lakshmi Reddy (a.k.a. Dr. Reddy) at the beach, Amagansett, NY, 2006.

RIGHT: Jen's first car on its last leg. This was just before it was completely destroyed in a fire department training exercise.

ABOVE: On Jen and Bill's wedding day, on the beach in front of the Don CeSar Hotel, St. Pete Beach, FL, April 12, 2008.

LEFT: Bill and his mom, Barbara, and their mother-son dance at the wedding.

ABOVE: Jen and her dad during the father-daughter dance.

RIGHT: Bill and Jen on their honeymoon . . . and the entire kitchen staff and waitstaff at Le Méridien Hotel, Bora Bora, April 23, 2008.

LEFT: On top of the Great Wall of China.

RIGHT: Will knew who his mom was before he met her in person.

LEFT: Our first meeting with Will at the foster care facility in Beijing, February 2013.

RIGHT: Will and the Flying Lion.

ABOVE: Rocky and Maggie celebrate Valentine's Day.

ABOVE: First family portrait.

RIGHT: Will playing a little soccer at a friend's house in the fall of 2014.

LEFT: Bill, Jen, and their daughter, Zoey, in the car on the way back to the hotel from the orphanage.

LEFT: Will and Zoey at the museum. They got a bit closer to each other as they got closer to the dinosaur skeletons.

RIGHT: Jen's parents, David and Judy, with Will and Zoey at the Thanksgiving Day Parade in Houston, 2014.

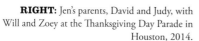

ABOVE: Zoey and Will digging into some shaved ice on a hot Houston day.

RIGHT: Zoey is rather excited about her cupcake.

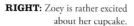

LEFT: Will and Zoey on their first day of school in 2015.

ABOVE: Jen delivering a keynote speech.

ABOVE: Dad and daughter selfie in the driveway, driving slow in Daddy's car, October 2015.

ABOVE: Jen's parents, David and Judy, with the kids at Halloween, 2015.

RIGHT: Bill's parents, Bill and Debbie, and all of the grandkids (as of December 2015 anyway).

Our conversation happened just a few months before I hurt my back, but I can picture the scene right now like it happened only moments ago. I was driving in my neighborhood, talking with Bobby on the phone, when he gave me a warning.

"Bill, you have to take care of yourself."

I had told him I was working out and getting back into shape. All I could do was laugh and shrug off his advice. Yet he knew I was a couple of years away from turning forty.

"Trust me, you're going to have to take care of yourself," Bobby told me. "Especially your back. You can't do any heavy lifting."

As I pulled into the driveway at our house, which had been newly built, I kept thinking what he was saying didn't really apply to me.

Ah, old man Bobby. He doesn't know how well I'm doing in the gym.

Three months later, I realized I listened to the wrong advice. Instead of listening to the warning about taking it easy with the kettle bell, I went ahead with more of it.

You live and you learn. Sometimes, you have to learn your limitations the hard way.

REALIZE YOUR CAPABILITIES

Jen

Unfortunately, medicine is not a perfect science. You can study hard, get top grades, train under the best of the best, and still fail to save a patient. It's part of the job. And a good doctor is able not just to learn from mistakes but to appreciate our limitations. There is only so much we can do.

I remember one particularly difficult evening where I lost two patients. Both were preterm babies with a multitude of complications. Not that the other 118 patients in the NICU were uncomplicated, but these little ones had a tremendous battle ahead of them. One that they would both lose.

The first was a baby who was diagnosed with intrauterine growth restriction (IUGR). The complications with this diagnosis include things like respiratory difficulty, nutritional limitations, and a weakened immune response, among other things.

On this night, just after arriving for my overnight shift, the baby went into respiratory and cardiac arrest. We worked tirelessly, employing every technique we could to save the patient, but we were, sadly, unsuccessful.

Shortly before the end of my twenty-four-hour shift, we received a call from the delivery room. They needed the neonatology team to respond to the impending birth of a preterm baby diagnosed with a congenital diaphragmatic hernia, which is a hole between the chest and abdomen that allows organs to pass through the hole and into the chest, restricting lung growth. For full-term babies, this complication is severe enough to make the survival rate only fifty to seventy-five percent. But for preterm babies, that rate can drop dramatically. Sadly, once the baby was born, despite an aggressive resuscitation, it became clear that this was a baby we could not save.

I don't know why these cases hit me so hard. I had seen cases like this many times before. But, on this occasion, I had a very tough time wrapping my head around losing these two patients. I reviewed and re-reviewed our process, the procedures, and notes. We did everything we were supposed to do. I sat in the call room (a room where you could go to get a few minutes of sleep between emergencies when working overnight) upset and doubting myself, when I remembered a note I had received from Dr. Kopits years ago when I graduated from Miami and had been accepted into medical school. It had been an encouragement back then, many years ago after working and studying so hard and finally accomplishing the goal of getting into medical school. Now, many years later, the words spoke to me even more.

My Darling Jennifer:

Remember—God is the healer and we are only his hands.

Remember that all you're going to learn in becoming a doctor is going to give you the tools to take care of patients. Remember—first and foremost—you're a caregiver, someone who should always heal with compassion. Don't ever let the rigors of medical school take that away from you. It's going to be a very grueling four years and they're going to try to beat out your humanism. Don't let that happen. That's the most valuable thing you can bring to your patients.

Dr. Kopits

I knew he had been right. Medical school had been tough and arduous. From the moment I began to study medicine up to the present, I had seen physicians who forgot why they were doing what they were doing. They had the knowledge and skills but they were lacking the very thing that made Dr. Kopits the example that he had been: compassion.

Something else washed over me and calmed me down as I sat there, wondering why we lost those two babies. Something Dr. Kopits had spent years teaching me. Humility is of key importance in our profession. No matter how well trained we are—and no matter how talented and gifted a doctor or surgeon we might be—we're going to find patients we cannot save, puzzles we can't solve, and problems we unfortunately cannot fix. The goal is always to save lives and solve puzzles and fix problems, but when that can't happen we have to learn how to be at peace with it. We have to be knowledgeable in our capabilities but also realize our limitations.

God is the healer and we are only his hands.

Some people are afraid of accepting limitations. They don't realize humility is a sign of strength. They can't fathom ever saying, "I don't know the answer to this, but I'm going to help you figure it out." They don't see the fact that people appreciate that sort of honesty.

Even the best and the brightest can't make miracles happen. Yet they can acknowledge the truth and work every day with the humility that it brings. I continue to try to do that, and I'm fortunate to have reminders like the one from Dr. Kopits when I need encouragement to keep going.

BE AWESOME

Bill and Jen

All of us grow up learning from experience. We learn from the things taught to us in school and by our parents, but also by what we see and encounter. We learned at a young age what hospitals looked like and what surgeries felt like and how the life of a Little Person had certain limitations. Some of these limitations were easy to accept, while others took time. We didn't give up right away on our hopes and dreams. Sometimes we had to adjust our circumstances and expectations.

The truth is every single one of us brings something to the table. We just have to believe in ourselves and *know* we can make a meaningful contribution.

Not everybody has an environment where they can thrive and grow. Some people might be physically and materially blessed, yet emotionally they have more scars than the two of us combined have from our surgeries. Knowing the reality of your life and what you can and can't do will only help on the road you're traveling.

Just remember: We're all awesome. You are awesome. We have to appreciate each other's gifts. Unfortunately, not everybody does. Especially in competitive environments like the business world or in the medical field, which are full of egos and a hunger to reach the top, at nearly any price.

Don't be afraid when some people don't appreciate or even know how awesome you are. Know your strengths and weaknesses as well as possible, and build something amazing around them.

KNOW THE FACTS

Here's another fun little exercise. You're doing these, right? If you haven't done any of them, please go back to Chapter One and start there. Okay, fine, you can keep going. But lists are fun—whether they're numbered lists and playlists or simply a list of random thoughts you email to yourself.

Make a list of the obvious limitations in your life. Don't put down things like "I can't swim as long as I want underwater" or "I don't think I'll marry Patrick Dempsey" or "I can't fly" (unless you're Maggie). Put limitations that hinder you from your goals. "I get nervous when I speak to crowds" or "I'm shy" or "I'm really terrible with numbers." It can be anything, stuff in your personal life or professional life, etc.

Here's an example from the stories in our book. Jen could have written years ago: "Will never be a marine biologist" or she could have put "Can't swim."

Now, after every limitation, write out something you *can* do in its place. Think of something that perhaps doesn't replace that limitation but that can allow you to possibly go around it and find something new. One of those *I can't do this* but *I can, however, do that.*

Jen, for instance, would have written "But I can go into medicine."

The list can build. A falling domino from Jen saying she can go into medicine would be "I will never be a trauma surgeon." And the answer to that would be "But there are other specialties I can focus on in the field of medicine" and then she could list them all.

Remember, you have to take the good with the bad. And if you take them both, as the theme song to that eighties show said, you have the facts of life.

Write up the facts of *your* life. Make the list. But for every bad make sure you have a corresponding good.

CHAPTER SIX

BELIEVE

"Optimism is the faith that leads to achievement.
Nothing can be done without hope and confidence."

—Helen Keller

BELIEVE IN MIRACLES

Bill

Believing can be a beautiful thing, especially when you can see the payoff. Super Bowl XLII is a really sweet example of that.

If you can't distinguish this particular Super Bowl from any of the rest because of the whole Roman numeral thing, that's okay. I'm sure it will shock you when I say my New York Giants were playing in this game. It was the championship for the 2007 NFL season played on February 3, 2008. The Giants were playing the New England Patriots.

The game hadn't been an explosion of points, but it also wasn't

a blowout like some of the Super Bowls we had seen in the last decade. It was quite a nail-biter, to be honest. Entering the fourth
quarter, the Patriots were ahead 7–3. The Giants were able to pull
ahead after quarterback Eli Manning threw a five-yard touchdown
pass to David Tyree.

With 11:05 left to play in the game, the Giants' 10–7 lead
wasn't something to sit back and relax on. And when you're playing against Tom Brady and the Patriots, that amount of time was
basically like an entire game. Sure enough, Brady marched his team
down the field and threw a touchdown pass to Randy Moss to make
it a 14–10 game (bad guys).

Now there were only two minutes and forty-two seconds left on
the clock.

I can only imagine what Eli Manning and the rest of the Giants
were feeling. I just know they weren't sitting back thinking to themselves *Well, gee, I really hope we win this.* Every single player and
coach on each team absolutely believed they were going to win. Yet
by the time the clock had stopped at 1:15 and it was 3rd and 5 on
the forty-four-yard line, that belief surely had to start waning a bit.

For the fans and the viewers out there, this game was both a
thrill and agony to watch. I was sharing a bottle of Johnnie Walker
Blue with my brother Joe . . . Okay, so he was sharing a bottle with
me, and we were feeling little pain. The whiskey was necessary, however, because this game was complete madness.

The final drive had already had so many jump-onto-the-couch-
and-scream moments to it. Giants wide receiver Amani Toomer
made two catches to continue the drive. The Giants would go for a

4th and 1 and just make it. Eli would have to scramble on the next play and would almost fumble while running. Then he nearly threw a game-ending interception on the sideline that thankfully slipped through the hands of the Patriots cornerback.

Fortune and fate were on the Giants' side on this day.

Everything was happening so quickly yet I feel like that next play took five minutes. I can still remember every single second of it. (Perhaps that's because I've viewed it on YouTube 1,472 times.) That play is not only seared on my memory and the memory of every Giants fan out there, but really on every single fan of football.

That play . . . Oh, that absolutely ridiculous play on 3rd and 5 with 1:15 remaining.

Eli Manning had been ticked off on the near interception, and the normally levelheaded quarterback was quite demonstrative with frustration. With the snap of the ball, Eli backed up but quickly was swallowed by linemen as the pocket around him collapsed. One of the Patriots linebackers nearly got to him but the Giants quarterback darted away from him. Then two other Patriots managed to grab his jersey, but somehow Eli slipped out of their clutches, running backward and almost tripping as he did. He had a second to drop back and plant his foot and then throw the bomb.

It was a long, smooth, sailing throw down the field to a Giant who was surrounded by three Patriots.

I felt as if I blacked out and suddenly woke up in a dream. But no—the miracle catch happened. Giants wide receiver David Tyree jumped off the field as if he was going for a basketball rebound rather than a football. Tyree caught the ball in both hands, but as he began to fall back to the grass, the ball and his hands kept falling behind his head, mostly due to Patriots safety Rodney Harrison trying to jerk the ball out of his grasp.

As both of them landed, Tyree somehow, in some incredible way, pressed the football in place against his helmet *with one hand* in order to keep possession of it. He would land squarely on his back on top of the Patriots player.

Joe and I went bonkers. And we knew then. Forget the Hail Mary pass. This one was the Hallelujah Chorus catch. We were believers. We knew, without a doubt, that the New York Giants had won. We were absolutely positive they would prevail.

The Giants would go ahead when Eli found wide receiver Plaxico Burress for a touchdown. The Patriots would have twenty-nine seconds to try to at least get a field goal and put it into overtime.

The New England Patriots were 18-0. They were undefeated. They had won three Super Bowls with Brady running the show.

We believe in you, Big Blue.

Nineteen seconds: 3rd and 20. A long bomb . . . Broken up.

Ten seconds now.

We have it.

Time to end the perfect season.

The throw by Brady on 4th down would sail a bit too far, ending that perfect record and answering our faith in our Giants.

What a crazy, joyous, and triumphant victory. And as I said, it felt this good because Joe and I and the Giants fans all believed. Every year, all NFL fans believe in their team. Miracles could happen. The 2007 Giants were an example of that.

In a lot of ways, Jen and I are examples of that, too. Despite some of those limitations we've talked about, and some of the outright no's, and the surgeries and the setbacks we've had, I think we're a lot like that 2007 New York Giants team.

It wasn't always perfect and it wasn't always pretty. But there have been some moving and miraculous moments we've gotten to share together. And it's the belief and the faith that they could come true that allowed them to happen in the first place.

BELIEVE IN YOU

Jen

I've always been pretty private about my own faith and beliefs. I grew up in that world, especially after my parents decided to transfer me from public to private Catholic school, St. Charles Borromeo Catholic School. I'm thankful my parents transferred me to St. Charles, as it was a good fit for me and my clear-cut, right-and-wrong personality. I grew to love school and its sense of respect and community. To be honest, I felt much more included at a place like this school than in the ever-expanding classes of Rolling Hills Elementary, where I had attended school for my first few scholarly years.

As I've grown older, faith has continued to be an important part of my life. I believe in religion and prayer, but I've never been as devout as I would like to be. Attending Sunday mass is something we normally do on holidays and special occasions. But still, I know how much faith can ground me.

I remember back in high school I had the occasion to question whether there was a God. Did we all get here because of a Big Bang, and what did that mean? As someone who spends many hours studying in the field of science, I know that faith can sometimes be relegated to a place below facts and data. And like so many others, there have been times when I've struggled with doubt.

I will share a few things about what I believe. After taking a look at my life, I believe that God has a plan. Whatever is meant to be will be. Moreover, I wouldn't dare pretend to be able to predict or understand what that plan might be.

And while my faith is important to me, it's not all that gets me through my tough times. I've clung on to hope and prayed for myself and my family. But the strength to move on and to keep going has to come from within.

The belief in pursuing a career, or in finding love, or in starting a family, or in the myth of a "happily ever after" comes from telling yourself that those things can indeed happen. Yet you're the one who has to *think* it and believe it. To go ahead and try and hope and then initiate the journey, rejecting the no's and accepting all you can know. If you don't believe in yourself and in the possibility of your dreams, it will be nearly impossible to achieve your goals.

Belief is looking ahead at the sunset with optimism, knowing that in order to follow it you have to get in the car and go.

UNIVERSAL BELIEF

- -

Bill

I've always held the belief that the right girl was out there for me and I would find her at the right time. Little did I know I'd been circling around her my whole life, like the way the Earth orbits around the sun. Yes, sure—that sounds like a Hallmark card sent by a third-grader. But as a reasonably bright man married to a far more brilliant doctor, I have scientific proof. Take Isaac Newton's Law of Universal Gravitation, which states the following: The force of gravitational attraction between two masses is inversely proportional to the square of the distance that separates them (generally speaking). Meaning, the closer the objects are to each other, the greater the attraction. If given enough time, they will collide.

Newton's Law of Universal Gravitation sure does make it easy to explain how Jen and I finally got together. We start off with two masses hurtling through time and space (that's me and Jen). When we met for the first time in the hospital at the young age of ten, the gravitational force, unbeknown to us, which had always been in place, began to exert a greater force of attraction on each other. In our early twenties, our nurse practitioner, twice, made attempts to connect us together, and our paths nearly intersect. We are now aware of each other but moving away from each other but within our respective orbits. We reach the outer limits of our orbit (also known as work, residency, and dating) and then begin the journey back toward each other. By the time we are in our early thirties, it would appear our orbit is about to turn into a collision. The gravitational force is too great to keep us apart any longer. Boom! We're married.

Okay . . . so science can't prove that the laws of physics and gravity somehow pulled the two of us together. But the way things worked out . . . I just know the universe was trying its best to play matchmaker from the moment we were born.

We've mentioned how as a kid I stumbled into Jennifer's hospital room while she was recovering from surgery and was not quite in the mood to become friends with a stranger. So she had ordered me out.

As many of you who know our story have heard, our hospital stays and surgeries would link us together. In college, a nurse practitioner named Diane who worked with Dr. Kopits even tried to set the two of us up. But we never ended up meeting until long after we graduated from college.

So while fate certainly seemed to be on our side when we both look back at it, there were still decisions and choices we were able to make. Dating, for instance, is something you get to control a bit. Well, at least you have the illusion of control. You're not stuck with a date like you are with your crazy uncle Eddie who talks about his hat collection nonstop. If things don't go well, you go home and don't call them again. End of story. You move on to the next profile, or the next friend of a friend, or whatever.

Belief plays a big part in dating and falling in love just like it does in every other aspect of life. For instance, if you want to win a gold medal in the Olympics, the first step is believing that you can win it. (And I hear there's lots of practicing involved, too.) If you want to own your dream car (which for me would be the

Porsche 356), then you have to believe you will be able to save up enough money to purchase it (or perhaps win a billion-dollar Powerball jackpot).

I've come to learn that to have success in dating, just like in any other area of life, you have to believe you can achieve the outcome you're hoping for. And going beyond that—finding that magical thing called love—is the same thing.

The first step toward finding the right person is believing they're out there to be found.

I know this because many years of trial and error have shown me it's true. Those same years have also shown me that it's easier said than done. Like most boys, I became interested in members of the opposite sex at an early age. I liked the idea of going on a date, but I had little clue as to what I was looking for in a girl.

Really . . . let's be honest. Most guys have little or no clue, right? (And I'm not saying that just because the publisher told me 87.45 percent of the readers of our books happen to be female!)

I always looked forward to school dances in junior high and high school. I would slick my hair back, put on my best baggy jeans and flannel shirt, and spray on some of my dad's cologne, Old Spice. My friends and I would then proceed to stand around in the school gym and watch people do the Cabbage Patch and the Butterfly, and, occasionally, an awkward slow dance that looked more like the lineup before a mass execution. The whole time my friends and I would try to work up the courage to talk to whatever girl we had our eye on.

Most of my friends were as awkward as I was, but a few had some success. They would talk with actual girls. Even dance with them. Occasionally, one would even ask a girl out and find a living, breathing girlfriend.

I wasn't so lucky. For me, dances were usually rather anticlimactic. In fact, as much as I looked forward to them, I also attended them partly so my absence would not be noticed. Like most kids, my goal was to blend in. It was a difficult time in my life because, as everyone else was growing at an alarming rate, the gap between me and my classmates continued to expand. It was becoming increasingly difficult to convince myself that I would ever find a girlfriend, let alone someday a wife.

My date for senior prom was a girl named Mary. She was one of those "she's just a friend" sort of dates. You know, the kind I would have to explain to my mom wasn't actually my girlfriend. We'd become friends over the prior couple of years and I thought it better to go to the prom with a friend than not go. That was about as close to dating as I got until I left for college.

It might shock you when I admit I was not the prom king. We had a lot of fun, but our mood didn't quite fit the prom song "Wonderful Tonight" by Eric Clapton. I wondered even then if I would ever slow-dance with anyone—not just a friend, but someone who actually had interest in me beyond friendship, someone I could stare at and sing every single word of Clapton's song to.

Back then, if I had to be truly honest, I would have told you I wasn't sure. I really did not know.

Mary and I took a limo into the city after the prom along with a few of my friends and their dates to go see a comedy act at Catch a Rising Star. Maybe there wasn't going to be love on prom night, but there could still be laughter. We had some beers and took the limo back to a friend's house where everyone crashed for the night.

Like so many kids, I had high hopes for college. There would be no more awkward growing pains. No more parents to report to. College was to be my emancipation from childhood and an opportunity to re-create my persona. I was sure I would have better luck with girls there.

College started off great. I attended NYU, where I majored in biology. I lived in Goddard Hall, a dormitory on Washington Square East. The dorms were co-ed, which meant there were girls everywhere! Unfortunately, I quickly found out that proximity would not increase my chances. I also discovered that, while the venue had changed, the mind-set of the "men and women" around me was not much different from high school. Sure, I was quick to make friends in my dorm and in my classes. But my dream that college would be an equalizer evaporated.

*Is the right person really out there?**

This wasn't just a question I was asking myself back then. It's a question everyone wonders. I just had to add a little asterisk to the question.

**And can they overlook my stature and disability?*

Like the Billy Joel song goes, I was keeping the faith. At least I was trying to. College, overall, was pretty good to me. And while there were some dark moments during that time, I also was able to find a bright spot in someone who took an interest in me. I would date a girl for a little more than a year. It was typical of a college romance, and I was grateful to have something typical in an otherwise atypical life. We would both eventually move on, knowing there was someone else out there meant for each of us.

It's easy to allow something you believed as a kid to suddenly begin to fade away a bit when you're busy starting a career in your twenties. Those years seemed to go by so fast. My dreams and goals for a career—many of which have been mentioned in this book— obviously were very important to me. Between long days in the office and a fair amount of travel to see clients, work dominated my time. Finding that special someone was still on my mind, but it just never happened. I would occasionally go on a date, but there were only one or two that I even considered moving beyond dinner and a movie.

By the time I was thirty, I had achieved several of the goals I had set for myself personally and professionally. I had been promoted a number of times at work and was making a good income. And on the personal side of things, I had purchased my first home. The significance to turning a decade older got my attention. I suddenly began to really wonder whether there might be someone out there with whom I'd share this home and this life.

The bar scene was never my thing. It was awkward for me to try to have a conversation when I was never speaking with a woman face-to-face. In addition to that, my friends never offered to set me up on a blind date. So when I heard about some of the great success stories from friends about online dating, I decided to go ahead and give it a shot.

Match.com here I come.

I began to register and wondered who would be the first woman I'd end up being in contact with. Where would I take her? How uncomfortable would it be? How much would I know about her?

The questions and curiosity stopped when I couldn't finish my profile. I was entering my data and when I got to the field for height, I was unable to enter my correct height. I guess they never envisioned a four-foot-tall man enlisting their services and I had some trepidation about lying on my profile, even if inadvertently. So I elected to skip publishing my profile.

Then I came across the website DateALittle.com. This was a site created specifically to connect people who were short in stature. I registered and created a profile and began my search.

It didn't take long before the Law of Gravity directed me to someone. When I came across Jennifer's profile, I swore that I knew her. Reading about her, I wondered if she was the one the nurse practitioner working with Dr. Kopits had tried to set me up with years ago.

Looking back on it, I don't think Jen would have liked the twenty-one-year-old version of Bill Klein. I had to grow up a bit and find myself. The years had taught me a lot. Everything happens for a reason, and I'm grateful that we met when the time was right.

Jennifer certainly seemed like an interesting character as I read about her on the website. She was pretty, obviously very intelligent—her profile said she was a doctor—and based on her interests and photos, it appeared she liked to have fun. So I took a chance and sent her a message.

I took a chance and had faith that maybe tomorrow I'd wake up and hear something from her. Or maybe the next day. Or the next.

A week later, I still had faith.

A week after that, I still . . . Well, I began to have some doubt.

A week after that, I began to think about going back on Match .com and telling people I was six feet four inches and weighed 240 pounds and played professional football for the New York Giants.

Yes, you have to believe. But sometimes it's hard. Sometimes it's almost impossible. But even after you close the door, sometimes you'll be surprised at the sudden knock you might hear in the background.

BELIEVE IN SERENDIPITY

Jen

Love can be as simple as two people grabbing for the same black cashmere gloves in a department store while Christmas shopping. A young man and young woman trying to buy a gift for their respective loves. After Jonathan and Sara introduce themselves and talk and spend a magical afternoon and evening together, the couple go to exchange numbers, but Sara wants to test fate out. She tells Jonathan to write his name and number on a five-dollar bill while she writes the same on the front page of the novel *Love in the Time of Cholera* by Gabriel García Márquez. If they're meant to be together, he will find the book or she will find the five dollars. This is the plotline that sets the stage in one of my favorite movies, *Serendipity*.

I've always been a big John Cusack fan and really liked the newly emerging actor, Kate Beckinsale, who plays Sara. I've loved this movie even though I realized what a crazy idea this is. Yes, it's a fairy tale. But a girl can love a well-told fairy tale, can't she?

When I was a young girl, I would dream about finding the love of my life. He would be sweet and funny and a perfect gentleman as well as cute and maybe a little bit of a geek. Our meeting might be as simple as the couple connecting in *Serendipity*. We could bump into each other and then talk and laugh and end up eating ice cream. Sparks could fly and the rest would be history.

Yet I couldn't help having a question interrupt those nice daydreams: Who's going to want to get on their knees in order to dance with their wife on their wedding day?

In my dreams, my stature played no role in my romance. Yet in real life, I couldn't do anything about the fact that I was a Little Person. I kept those dreams in my head and my heart, and I also tried to silence the voices that told me it would never happen.

I knew I had to keep believing for that dance to ever take place. If I stopped believing, then it would most certainly never happen.

One dance that did take place was during my years of medical school. Dancing with Snorey would be a big moment in my life, and it wasn't because he was well over six feet tall. He was a classmate of mine from Norway. A very tall classmate. All of our friends would love to put us together and then say, "Look! Aren't they soooo cute!" And yes, I understood. They were basically saying, "Look! It's the tallest guy around with the shortest girl!"

I never took offense and had fun with it, though it was a bit strange, especially since we weren't that close. But dancing with Snorey was me trying to get out there and have fun and hang on to the belief of finding love. I wanted to find that great love of my life. Of course, by saying "great" I didn't necessarily mean "very large" or "towering over me." But I had made this an important personal goal of mine, and I didn't want to rule out anything. Even extremely tall Norwegians.

I chose to do what Kate Beckinsale's character in *Serendipity* says to do. There's a sweet scene where this couple finally bids farewell to each other after that magical first night when they meet. They make another bet by the elevators in a hotel lobby. Sara tells Jonathan they'll each get into an elevator and choose one floor. If they both choose the same one, then they're meant to be together. The guy, played to perfection by the magnificent John Cusack, is completely perplexed and tells her he doesn't understand why she's doing all of this.

"You don't have to understand," Sara tells Jonathan. "You just have to have faith."

"Faith in what?" he asks.

"Destiny."

I've always loved those lines. They fit, too, with the way I look at things. You have to believe things will work out. Yet you also have to go ahead and press the floor number and then watch the doors open on the new floor to see what happens.

So I simply waited for someone to come along whom I could tempt fate with. Someone I could play that elevator game with, or maybe just hold hands with as we rode the same elevator up to wherever it might take us. I chose to believe my own serendipity would show up.

I believed. And I kept believing. I worked hard and dreamed big and managed to stay very, very busy. But I believed and never stopped. I blinked and my twenties suddenly disappeared. Yet when

I reached my thirties, that belief was still there. Sometimes I'd force myself to be more proactive. To go to the parties, to hang out with my colleagues, and to get out there, all in the hope that maybe my true love would find me. Maybe I'd suddenly spot him in the middle of the crowd, or he'd bump into me as we were crossing an intersection, or we'd get caught in a thunderstorm and find ourselves to be the only two customers in a rundown coffee shop that was for sale by its owner and needed renovating just like our love lives.

There's nothing wrong with adding a little romance to your beliefs.

I didn't just get out there with my friends and colleagues—I was actually the party planner. That turned out to be a great thing because when the slow songs came on and couples began to dance together, I always had something to do, like check on the DJ or make sure all the food was put out. That way I didn't have to sit awkwardly on the sidelines watching all the romance on the dance floor and in the air.

This belief would eventually lead to my signing up on DateA Little.com, as I already mentioned. It would also prompt me, with just a bit of help from my best friend, Lakshmi, to contact someone directly. To put myself out there and be willing to risk something. I wasn't risking *everything*. At the most, I was just risking being ignored and never being replied to.

While a typical night of hanging out with Lakshmi meant watching *Sex and the City* over a glass of wine, this night meant actually trying to pursue it. She had put parameters around her search for men to within a fifty-mile radius. I, on the other hand, decided to be a little more generous. I made my search in a five-hundred-mile radius. The truth was, searching within a fifty-mile radius would have resulted in very few people, ones I would have likely met at the regional meetings LPA had held.

I wanted to find someone new, someone who didn't know anybody in my circle of friends, someone who had only lived in the corners of my dreams.

Someone like him.

The picture on the screen stopped me for the moment.

The someone I found, the man I chose to email, was handsome, with blue eyes. His picture showed him piloting a boat while his profile showed him having a job. The former piqued my curiosity while the latter made me comfortable enough to send him a message, knowing he wasn't a slacker.

To send *Bill Klein from Long Island* a message.

So we emailed each other and then spoke on the phone and I was enjoying getting to know Bill until two months later he revealed the truth.

"You know, I actually have to tell you something," he said. "I know you."

"You do?" I asked.

"Yeah. I've been following your career. Ever since you went to medical school."

My internal stalker sirens suddenly began to go off. I was wondering what I had gotten myself into.

Good thing you're up there in New York and I'm in Pittsburgh.

Yet Bill explained *how* he knew me. And the story he told might as well have been as unlikely as Sara and Jonathan meeting in the movie. Except in this screenplay our heroine was a young Little Person recovering from surgery feeling lonely and in a lot of pain. Our hero, on the other hand, was also a Little Person around the same age. He ended up rushing into her hospital room greeting her only to be ordered out.

I didn't believe it, of course. I didn't remember it. Yet I asked him about other patients who had been at the hospital and about doctors and nurses and details and he knew them all. He shared memories of *my* childhood, this man I only knew from our phone calls and the dashing snapshot of him in that boat.

"How did you know that?" I asked.

"Well, I was there," Bill said. "And I have a pretty good memory."

Forget randomly meeting in a department store while Christmas shopping. That's so predictable. But the ten-year-old boy in a wheelchair being kicked out of a hospital room because another patient—*this* particular patient—hadn't been feeling well and her mother told him to leave?

Bill shared about how we almost met in college after the International Center for Skeletal Dysplasia's nurse practitioner and close family friend tried to set us up, but how he had been too busy, much like me. He shared how he ended up spending a summer shadowing Dr. Kopits a year after I had. He had fallen in love with medicine much like I had. Growing up in a hospital and growing up around surgeons and nurses and physical therapists can do that to someone. While he hadn't continued to pursue a career in this field, we still held that mutual interest.

That and about a hundred others.

For two decades now, Bill and I had been like ships passing in the night. We had been in the same waters, however, and sometimes we had even been set adrift far out to sea.

Fate didn't mean for us to come together back then. God would give us the ability to make the choices we did to eventually find ourselves spending moments talking on the phone. It was up to Bill and me, however, to seize those moments.

Perhaps "seize" shouldn't be the word I use for some of those conversations. Especially the one at night where, after a long week at work, I fell asleep while on the phone with Bill. Maybe "snooze" is the right word. He had a voice you didn't mind listening to and he enjoyed sharing anecdotes about life. I guess on this night, his bedtime story worked. I was out. But this prompted him to finally decide that there had been enough chatting on the phone. Bill wanted to officially meet for the "first" time.

When we finally did meet in person, I knew. I had believed that my true love was out there for so long, and now I just knew I had found him.

BELIEVE IT CAN HAPPEN

Bill

Taking any sort of leap of faith is a daunting thing, no matter why you're doing it. The more you have to lose, the more fearful you can be. If it's a bank account you might bust, then you can simply tell yourself it's just money. If it's a business you've spent years building only to go broke, then it's harder to accept the fall. But if it's your heart that's going to break—one that's already been bruised and scarred by a lifetime of ignorance and solitude and being set apart from everyone else—then placing it out there is all the more difficult.

Jennifer Arnold was worth the risk.

I realized after hearing snoring on the other line of the phone in the middle of one of my sentences that we were becoming very comfortable in our dialogue. Perhaps a bit *too* comfortable. It's one thing to be sitting on a love seat; I didn't want to be on the easy chair. It was time to move our relationship forward.

We discussed what would be the most ideal weekend for a first date. Jennifer's calendar was pretty filled up, leaving only her birthday weekend available for me to travel to Pittsburgh. I knew flying over to meet Jen for the first time on her birthday might seem to be a bit much—to be moving too quickly—but I wanted to make a statement. I wanted to literally sweep her off her feet.

I rented a hotel room and flew to Pittsburgh on March 10, 2006. I was so nervous for our first meeting. I hoped it would go well and that she would like me as much as I liked her.

We decided to meet after she got off work so we could go grab some coffee. Yes, hopping onto a plane and flying in and renting a hotel room all for . . . coffee? The fact of the matter is, we could have been in the best restaurant or in the back of a cab. We wouldn't have noticed anyway. We were too focused on each other.

I've shared some of these details before, but they bear repeating. The first thing I recall is standing on a sidewalk and hearing that horrible rumbling sound. The noise of a vehicle screaming in despair, asking to be taken out back and shot. Then I saw the snow-salt-coated gray KIA Sportage rounding the corner, only to realize it was actually white but was in desperate need of a car wash. As a car aficionado, I looked at the approaching vehicle in a slight state of terror.

Geez, I hope this isn't . . .

Then I saw her. The woman behind the wheel, the image resembling the photo I had memorized. She wasn't posing but she was smiling and she was real and in person and she was driving toward me. Suddenly, everything else disappeared. Any silly thought about her car or anything else was silenced.

If you have never been fortunate enough to fall in love at first sight, then you won't fully understand this moment for me. If you have, you'll understand the amazement flowing through my body, through every part of my being. I held my breath and watched her approaching and smiled and had a hundred different thoughts all summed up by one.

I've been waiting for you my whole life and you're finally driving up as if you've been planning to all along.

If I took my eyes off her, the spell might break, so I didn't. I simply opened the door of the SUV and climbed in. What do you say to the love of your life, the woman of your dreams, your future wife and the mother of your two future children?

I think I managed to say a "Hi, love your car."

Like many great romances of the twenty-first century, we chose to have our first date at Starbucks. It was expensive enough to feel like it was worthy of our meeting, and the coffee was hot enough to scald me if I suddenly turned out to be a major creeper. We sat down with our two cups of coffee and a hundred stories and spoke for three hours. Jen and I spoke about everything. And I couldn't escape the obvious.

I've known you my whole life.

I hadn't, in fact, known her, yet it felt like I had—our connections and our chemistry. The way she laughed at my jokes even when they weren't quite funny. The way she seemed to be completely brilliant yet unable to make a decision about whether to get another cup of coffee or not. We both shared details about our families, our closest friends, our careers, and our interests.

After she brought me back to my hotel, I thanked her for the amazing afternoon and for driving. Then I gave her a small kiss on the cheek and we parted ways until dinner that evening.

I am a good salesman (salesmen need to be modest, and that's why I say "good," because really in truth I'm a spectacular salesman), and I am me ("Klein. Bill Klein."), which means I'm never searching for words. Yet after Jen picked me up later that evening, amazingly enough in that same ugly SUV, I found myself thankful she showed up for the date. She could have been polite but then gotten back home only to think, How can I end this? I also found myself wondering if we would have much else to say to each other since we had already talked all afternoon.

Since we both loved sushi, we went to a sushi place. I decided to go ahead and order almost everything on the menu. Jen and I sat at the table and talked and talked more. We ended up eating nothing. Even the sushi chef couldn't believe it. After "dinner," we paid the bill and started to walk out. He asked us why we hadn't eaten anything. We both responded in unison:

"We were just talking."

Who had time to eat when you had to catch up on three decades of life?

Truth be known, Jen confessed later while devouring some chips that she wasn't a big sushi eater. She was being polite. Looks like my life might be filled with tables for one at the sushi bar when Jen's working an overnight call at the hospital.

The most magical moment of the weekend came that evening when Jennifer drove me across the Monongahela River up to Mount Washington for a view of Pittsburgh. We walked out onto the overlook where we could see the entire city glowing like some sort of ornately decorated Christmas tree. The glittering skyscrapers and bridges reflected off the surface of the river, resembling dozens of candles lit in the distance.

Since it was cold outside, Jen stood there shivering with the wind whipping around us. I put my arms around her, basically stuffing her into my overcoat with me. We looked so cute. I just wanted to keep her warm, of course. So naturally, a kiss only helped keep her blood flowing. I was only trying to help a freezing lady out.

We don't have to strain to believe the sun will rise each morning. Even on those dark, rainy days, we know the sun is up there behind the clouds. Neither do we have to force ourselves to believe whether that same sun will set. It always does, regardless of what sort of day you've had. Whether you're staring at the fading light from the porch on your house or from a window in your hospital room, you still always know it's going to set.

Standing and looking out to the glowing majesty in front of us, I realized it was as easy to believe in love as it was to know the sun would rise and set. I knew I had to believe in it the same way I knew all those lights would illuminate the city glowing in the distance.

This would be the start of something really wonderful. The beginning of another journey. This particular one would be incredible since I had someone to share it with. Someone who had also never given up believing it could happen.

BELIEVE EVEN WHEN IT'S HARD

Jen

The hope of finding the love of my life was finally answered when I met Bill. It was confirmed when we married on April 12, 2008, in the St. Mary Our Lady of Grace Catholic Church in downtown St. Petersburg, Florida. The event and the honeymoon were amazing whirlwinds that felt like gifts given to us for being persistent and never giving up.

With the start of our show and with the world being able to

watch our lives unfold before them on *The Little Couple*, we were able to begin to live the dream. The two of us were busy professionals pursuing careers we had worked hard for. We were able to build our dream house. Our first two children were Rocky and Maggie. Life looked good and so many wonderful things were happening for us.

As we'll share more in the last two chapters, Thinking Big isn't a map to get you to a certain destination. Besides, it's about the journey and not the destination anyway, as we always say. These values and ways of looking at the world weren't planned out in order for us to find the right job or the right partner or to move into the right house and then drive off into the right sunset. Certainly not. Instead, they've been tools we've used since we were young.

And with life being the unpredictable thing it can be, Bill and I would discover we would have to keep using these principles on the road we were about to travel. We would truly learn what it meant to overcome obstacles with optimism.

Our journey toward having a family took us from questioning whether I should become pregnant the natural way to then going the surrogacy route instead. After our wonderful surrogate, a woman named Cindy, miscarried around eight weeks into our first pregnancy, Bill and I naturally were devastated. Yet I knew right away not to give up. We had only tried once. We don't give up that easily. That's not who we are.

You don't accomplish something to prove a point or to be proud of yourself. Rather it's about seeking out joy and hope in the world.

Sometimes it's about not giving up. Every day is a search for happiness, whether it's by attempting to do something for yourself and your family or it's by helping others in the same sort of capacity.

After Cindy miscarried for a second time after only ten days, keeping the faith felt a little more difficult for Bill and me. Although it was only our second transfer and miscarriage, it took five egg retrievals to get to that one transfer. It was around Christmastime, so the news was especially tough considering the timing. Thankfully, we had other people around to push up our spirits and pull us along with them. Although the spirit to keep trying was still there, I was starting to realize that maybe it was time to move in a different direction.

We had been on a journey of trying to start a family for almost two years. Once again, I knew we couldn't give up. We both still believed.

Belief allows you to stay open to new possibilities. To go ahead and do things like putting your name on a list for adoption even when you have no idea if you'll go that route. Only two and a half months after this second loss, we heard there was a child available for an international adoption. It would have been easy to say "Not now, I'm still grieving." To let the dust settle before deciding to take another risk. But that's not an option when you truly believe in something.

If you stay the course and are optimistic, you might find yourself seeing joy in your hands. Bill and I would end up doing this when we first saw pictures of an adorable two-year-old boy from Hohhot, the capital of Inner Mongolia. He had been born with skeletal dysplasia and we were told he wasn't in the best of health due to his care earlier in his life. Yet his smile said it all.

You know I'm worth flying halfway around the world to meet, he seemed to say.

Of course, this was our beloved Will. And then, hope knocked on our door soon afterward. It felt a bit like having the Girl Scout cookies delivered to your door, only to hear the knocking again an hour later and being given another armload of goodies.

Obviously, this second child was Zoey. Her photo showed her big, beautiful eyes. We needed to bring her home to be a part of our family. Those trips to meet our children and pick them up were detailed in our first book. Joy rushed over us in ways we hadn't expected and surely couldn't have imagined so soon after our experiences with surrogacy. We believed we could become parents, and our faith was answered.

Of course, it wasn't all smooth sailing. You already know that I flew home from India early and was diagnosed with cancer shortly thereafter. We were filled with so many questions:

Will has been with us for a while and we just met Zoey—why now?

After all the surgeries and the disappointments and the heartache, how can this be happening? What many people can forget about Bill and me is that much of our lives has been punctuated with moments like that. Do we wish our lives hadn't been? Of course. But that was our life. Our fate or destiny or however you want to put it. Yet as my mother and my aunt taught me growing up, I could not wallow in self-pity. There was no point. It would do me no good. Feeling sorry for myself wasn't going to make me grow when

I was younger. Any sort of woe-is-me attitude wasn't going to prevent those surgeries from helping with my skeletal dysplasia. I knew being angry or bitter would not make the cancer go away. I knew it would simply be another form of cancer inside of me. I already had one I had to fight, so why have another?

The irony of the situation was almost surreal . . . I know that terrible things can happen to people at the most unexpected and inopportune times. That is what I see every day in my work—new parents so excited at the beginning of parenthood, filled with hope for their unborn baby, who suddenly have their whole life turned upside down when they find out there's a life-threatening situation. So I started realizing that my question of "why me, why now?" should really be "why not me, why not now?"

I knew I had to believe that I would beat the disease. Despite what Bill might say, I am not a superhero. I needed to be strong and get through the surgery and believe things were going to be fine. I had to be resilient, and I had plenty of practice at that, so I simply believed I would come through this. I knew that was the only option I wanted to believe in.

People sometimes ask how I've managed to stay positive. How we've stayed so strong. It's a discipline we have acquired over time. We've had more than forty years of experiential training to help us create a mind-set of faith.

Hopefully, you've been able to have a life without too many great setbacks. But maybe even now you're suddenly in the middle of the cyclone, staring at the winds circling you, wondering how in the world you're going to ever get out of it.

You have to choose to have faith that things will get better. You have to believe that those storms surrounding you will eventually die down. Like every great doctor or athlete or businessperson or inventor or artist, you have to know you can ultimately have victory in whatever sort of battle you're facing.

I'm grateful I was able to eventually share with the world the following tweet:

It's official—ME 1 vs CANCER 0 . . . I WIN!

DON'T STOP BELIEVIN'

Bill

There's nothing like demonstrating your parenting skills on national television. Especially when your daughter wants absolutely *nothing* to do with you. When she won't stop crying and won't look your way and will pull her hand away when you try to hold it.

I guess the daddy-daughter dance has to wait until . . . Well, I will wait no matter how long it takes.

There are some good reasons for why Zoey didn't instantly fall in love with me like she did with her mom. The orphanage she had been living in since her first week of life took care of young children and women under the age of seventeen. It was very likely Zoey had had little interaction with men in her life. Of course, that didn't help me feel much better nor instill confidence that I would one day overcome the obstacle of winning her trust, respect, and love. Everything we had been told about what to expect and how to prepare ourselves from an emotional perspective when we adopted Will came back to me. Before we adopted our son, we had been counseled about the resistance we might get and how it would be easy to doubt ourselves. Yet Will's transition was virtually instantaneous and permanent. It was unlike anything we had been warned about or anything described in the adoption literature.

It would take Zoey just a little more time before she began to accept me.

I was hoping Zoey's transition would be less bumpy. Not for me, but for her. On the plane ride back home, Zoey wouldn't sit beside me. I was so happy to hear her giggling in the seat behind me, especially since she has this fantastic laugh. I would peek over the seat and those bright eyes would catch mine and then she would flip the switch and shut down again. As far as she was concerned, I was the strange guy who had taken her out of her environment. And she wasn't wrong. To make things worse, the pretty lady who had been with the strange guy suddenly disappeared, leaving only the strange guy and the smiling boy.

This particular story of my first breakthrough with Zoey could have probably come in any of the chapters for this book, but I saved it for here, because it taught me something about the power of belief.

I knew that if I was going to make a connection with Zoey, it would have to be on her terms. I had to keep trying and to keep hoping that one day, her fears would be replaced by joy. I believed they would. I absolutely had to believe, in the same way Jen had to keep the faith while battling cancer. There was no other choice.

Throughout the adoption process, we had been encouraged to immerse ourselves in the kids. The experts told us to isolate ourselves—to basically lock ourselves in with our child—to help build that bond. This would allow for permanence to grow in the child and for them to believe that we weren't going anywhere. This was why the camera crew only filmed our initial arrival when we got back just to see Zoey's reaction to her new home. After that, the camera crew and everybody else was ordered to stay away. For a while, Mommy had to stay away as well.

Jen stayed with her parents while she was going through chemotherapy. Then she had surgery and stayed in the hospital. Eventually she came back home, but we still operated in triage mode. I was afraid Jen might need to go to the hospital in an emergency and, with the kids in separate bedrooms, a quick dash to the car would be all the more difficult. So, at nighttime, we all slept in our master bedroom. When we had first gotten Will, we would sleep with him in his room as he transitioned. Now that Jen was sick and had to sleep in our bed, we had to have Zoey there with us. So Will slept on a mattress with sheets, pillows, and a small bear-shaped blanket. Zoey was on the other side of our bed, in a larger than normal crib/pack-and-play, outfitted with a mattress, sheets, and stuffed animals galore.

Every night I would help get everybody in bed, and before I turned out the lights I would tell Zoey good night. With a simple look, she let me know there was nothing good about it, thank you very much. Yet I kept trying. I wasn't going to give up. Mommy, who was in bed recovering, wasn't giving up, so I couldn't either. I would do a nightly ritual where I'd work my way to the floor and lie next to Zoey's crib. I would put my hand up on the soft mesh wall between us, and every night Zoey would ignore it.

I'm not giving up, little lady.

I had seen where Zoey had been born and where she had been living. I knew I had to earn her trust. I would have gladly taken on those fears myself, just as I would have rather been the one fending off cancer and allowing Jen to bond with her daughter. But this was our situation, and all I could do was to keep trying.

Before we would go to bed at night, I would look down at her and wish she knew how her daddy felt. I wished I could make her believe she didn't have to be afraid. We had found her through a series of miracles. And she was meant to be with Jen and Will and me. I wish she could have known all the intense love we already had for her. But for now, she was scared and confused. I would look at that tiny face with its fierce expression. She was ours to help shape and mold and love and protect. I wanted her to believe I'm an okay guy. One who was going to take care of her in every way I could.

For now, all I could do was believe, and let her know I wasn't going anywhere by putting my hand on the wall of the playpen.

One night while we were getting ready for bed in the muted shadows of our bedroom, I knelt on the floor beside the crib and placed my hand on the mesh fabric. On this particular evening, something was different. Zoey moved over and reached out toward me with her hand, placing it against mine.

Then she did something else, something remarkable. She began to trace the outline of my hand with her little finger. I watched her in silence and with a huge smile and I didn't even realize I'd gotten teary-eyed. I turned to see if Jen was watching. She was witnessing the whole thing.

It didn't last long, but it was something. It was enough. It's all about baby steps, right? Zoey wasn't a baby anymore, but she was still a toddler. She had a long way to go. But so did our whole family.

I tried to hold on to this magical moment.

"Watch," I told Jen. "Tomorrow this will all be gone and we will have to start all over again."

Sure enough, the next morning Zoey didn't want to have anything to do with me. The temporary trust had evaporated. Yet every night, this became our thing. I would put my hand up to the wall of her playpen and hold it there, and she would do the same and then trace my fingers. She still had that security wall that made her feel safe enough to believe I couldn't get through. Soon enough I started putting my face against the mesh, and I felt her fingers circle my face.

Not long after the breakthrough with Zoey, I found myself driving down the road jamming to the Journey song "Don't Stop Believin'"—a song from my very first vinyl record. As the song I'd heard hundreds of times before began to play, I turned it up and listened to those initial lyrics. It felt like I was listening to this song for the first time.

"Just a small-town girl, livin' in a lonely world," Steve Perry sang.

The words suddenly took on a whole new meaning. I couldn't help thinking of our little Zoey suddenly being swooped up by these strangers and taken away in the night. She really had been a small-town girl living in a lonely world.

I pictured myself one day down the road with her. I imagined this beautiful teenage girl dealing with the pressures of adolescence and also the added stress of being a Little Person. I imagined picking her up from school and seeing the vulnerability on her face after some incident hurt her feelings. Then I imagined her trusting me enough to tell me what was wrong. Perhaps asking me to hold her hand. I believe that will happen someday.

When that day comes, there are a lot of things I might say to comfort her. But also, I will tell her to never give up. If she feels like life was really, *really* terrible that day, I'd encourage her to believe in tomorrow. Then maybe I'll crank up some more Steve Perry on our way home.

GET BUSY

Jen and Bill

It's no surprise that *The Shawshank Redemption* ranks up there with the most-beloved films of all time. Everything about the film is great cinema: an inspiring story that continues to surprise you along the way, great acting and cinematography and directing and an amazing score. Those things all help make it so loved, but the reason it really resonates with people is because it's all about hope.

We all remember the prison escape and the ending, where the character of Red finally gets released from prison and ends up finding his buddy Andy Dufresne on a beach down in Mexico. But the best part of the film might be a conversation between Red and Andy. It's where they talk about getting out of prison and about hopes and dreams.

Andy, the ever-optimist played by Tim Robbins, shares with his friend where he would go if he ever got out of Shawshank Prison. He would go to a little place on the Pacific Ocean called Zihuatanejo and live there for the rest of his life. Andy would open a hotel on the beach and fix up an old boat and entertain and take friends out fishing.

Red, however, doesn't share Andy's idealism. We see his complete sense of desperation as portrayed by the incredible Morgan Freeman. The actor has perhaps never been better. We see Red has given up on ever leaving the stone walls that confine him.

Red tells Andy he shouldn't be talking this way, he shouldn't be doing that to himself, that those thoughts are "s****y pipe dreams." That's the way it is, Red tells him. But Andy seems angry and defiant and delivers the defining line of the movie: "I guess it comes down to a simple choice, really. Get busy living or get busy dying."

The first-time viewer only knows what Red knows when Andy says this, but of course Andy has a few tricks up his sleeve. This whole conversation is an illustration of how you can look at life. Not just with the whole "get busy living or get busy dying" line, but rather in the discussion of hopes and dreams. Red believes Andy is talking about some far-fetched dream that's never going to happen, and because it won't he should just shut up. But Andy thinks differently.

For Andy, Zihuatanejo is not a pipe dream. It's hope. And while he hasn't stepped foot on that beach yet, he *believes* he will be able to one day. And as we will see, he's worked very, *very* hard to make it happen.

You might have heard this line about living and dying so many times that it no longer has any sort of impact on you. The same thing can be said about a song like "Don't Stop Believin'." And sure, they have been used many times as ways to share optimism and to encourage never giving up.

For us, the choice between living and dying never gets old. The encouragement to never stop believing never gets ignored. Because our whole lives have been about choosing day after day to get busy in some way. We've been facing those choices as long as we can remember.

There's a difference between conjuring up pipe dreams and holding on to belief.

We encourage you in your own journey to never stop believing, whether it's in love or your career or your art or your family or your faith. Believing in yourself means getting busy living. And you do that by Thinking Big.

CHAPTER SEVEN

IMPROVE

*"Whatever challenges you pick up in life, you can never decide
'I know enough.' You've got to keep pressing the boundaries."*
—Gene Kranz

ALLOW OTHERS TO IMPROVE

Jen

Life is a series of improvements. At least, we try for it to work out
that way. For example, hopefully our handwriting improves from
kindergarten to eighth grade, though of course it usually gets worse
once we're out of school. (Especially if you're a doctor—or an au-
thor signing books or anyone who has migrated to a computer and
away from a pen and pad.) We improve in knowledge, in skills,
in maturity, and in our social graces. As we become older, we can
begin to try to learn new things and become better people. Marriage
introduces new challenges, and optimistically the whole two-is-

better-than-one thing works in your favor. Then you introduce parenthood, which suddenly means you're now also trying to improve a
child or children who are growing up under your guidance.

In the previous chapter, we spoke about the idea of believing
in something. One example we gave was having hope about finding love. Thankfully, that's exactly what happened with Bill and me.
And even though this shouldn't have been a surprise, a wonderful
result of Bill coming into my life was that certain parts of my life
began to improve. Some *vastly* improved.

I'll share a story we haven't told before, one that shows a whole
other side to me. It was when Bill and I first began dating. He
would travel to Pittsburgh to see me and would stay with me during
the time we had together. I would learn very quickly that Bill likes
to get things done, and he is also very efficient and orderly about
it. In the second or third month we had been dating, he was staying with me and saw the mountain of laundry I needed to do, so
he volunteered to help me out. My town house had two stories and
a basement. And while the washer and dryer were in the basement,
most of my dirties were abandoned two flights of stairs up, so Bill
gladly went up and down those stairs for me.

As he was helping with the laundry, Bill came up to me with a
puzzled look on his face.

"Hey, Jen—what's with the bag of unopened envelopes?"

Ah, he had found my stash.

"That's just the mail," I told him.

"What kind of mail?" he asked, looking even more puzzled.

"All of it."

He could only laugh and shake his head. "You probably need to read some of it. Some of those letters are red, and it's not even Christmas."

"I know, I know. Work has been tough. You can see how well I've done with the laundry."

I would regularly work eighty to a hundred hours a week, and laundry and dishes would accrue during that time. I didn't have time to even look at the domestic stuff. Bill still looked perplexed, but a grin started to appear.

"You can put off laundry. Bills are another thing."

"I have enough money to get by, but I haven't had the time to pay them. And frankly, I could use a couple more days for my next paycheck to pay a couple of them, too."

"I can help if you want," Bill offered.

It sounded like an incredible idea.

"Well, if you don't mind just opening up all my mail, I'd really appreciate it."

Bill didn't mind helping me out, but he did mind seeing the first notices and second notices and final notices on everything from credit card statements to electricity bills. After going through them, Bill decided he had to find a solution.

"Jen, we have to fix this," he told me. "I can write out the checks to pay the bills."

Yes, not only do I have a boyfriend, now he's my sugar daddy!

This wasn't exactly my thought. Instead, I could only thank Bill.

"I'll pay you back," I said.

He knew I would, and he also knew that everything in my life at that point was about my job. In many ways, nothing else mattered to me, not even doing laundry or paying bills. My family and my hospital and my patients all mattered. And those are all great things.

Having Bill come into my life, however, was priceless. There were things about him that complemented me, and that improved my life. Love wasn't just some swelling emotion inside of you. It was him helping me and making my life easier. Hopefully, I've done the same for Bill since we've been together.

This was why when he ended up finally going on to improve himself, I couldn't help being emotional. He had been putting off back surgery for a while after his kettle bell injury, and now he was finally going to have the surgery done. But the surgery was complicated, and there were serious risks involved. I knew the risks better than most. Bill hadn't had surgery in a long time, so it brought a haunting question to mind: How many of these can we actually go through and come out on the other side?

As a kid I had always dreamed of finding the guy who loved me. But finding one who also did my laundry and balanced my checkbook? And was an amazing husband and father? I had found the love of my life and I didn't want to lose him. Memories of my childhood were suddenly brought back up. In many ways, I was more nervous about Bill going into surgery than I had been for my cancer treatment.

ACCEPT THE NECESSARY IMPROVEMENTS

Bill

My original idea for the second book I wanted to write was an exercise book. I was calling it *Body by Bill.* I'm still not sure why Simon & Schuster didn't go for it. *Note sarcasm.*

When I finally decided to improve my broken body and get my back checked out, it was obvious I needed to go ahead and have the surgery. So on October 20, 2014, I went for the complex surgery. As Jen knew, it was one of those dangerous, life-threatening surgeries. The measure of success would be variable and unpredictable. Success might look like getting only half of the results we'd want. This had a lot to do with all the variables. When a surgeon finally got inside to check out my back, he would finally see all the things he was dealing with. And even then, we would still need a little bit of luck for the surgery to go well.

The good news: The surgery arrested the progression of the disc intruding into my spinal cord. The bad news: The surgery was unable to remove the pain associated with the damage that had been done. My back still hurts, and the pain is fairly constant, but it's not an explosion of lightning through my body.

While in surgery, I ended up losing a lot of blood. And when I say a lot, I mean I lost half of the blood in my body. I would be on a vent for twenty-four hours while getting transfusions. Jen was about as terrified as a doctor wearing a wife hat could be. She didn't expect that much blood loss, or the complications post-op that kept me in the ICU longer than anyone wanted. Once, I woke up with the endotracheal tube in my mouth. This wasn't supposed to happen, and I know because when I later told the physician, he said I wasn't supposed to remember that. But I do. When I woke up, I felt like I was choking to death. And I wasn't breathing; the ventilator was doing it for me. For a few horrific seconds, I tried to get someone's attention, since I had a crowd of doctors and nurses hovering over me.

A little help here? Hello? Anybody?

Of course, I couldn't speak a word—after all, I had a huge tube down my throat. Either they knew what was going on and I was fine, or I was dead. Either the machine was working or it wasn't.

Yeah, fun stuff.

Over the next few days, I began my migration toward being discharged. After being moved to the ICU and then to the Orthopedic ICU, I got my own room and began to be able to stand up and take some steps.

Improving yourself in life sometimes is a real . . . Well, I want to keep this a family-friendly book. So I'll just say it's a real bear. Surgery is never fun, and then you go back home and slowly try to recover. You lie on your back to get some rest and the forty-plus stitches poke into you like little lumps of pain. You prop yourself up on a pillow to lie on your side and your arm falls asleep. You want to lie on your stomach but the metal rods in your back prevent you from ever being able to do that comfortably again.

The home health nurse I had tending to my wound and monitoring my progress once I arrived home in Houston was very nice. Nice, but very straightforward. She was the kind of nurse that you knew had seen a lot of whiners in her thirty-plus years on the job and wasn't about to put up with one more. Think Nurse Ratched from *One Flew Over the Cuckoo's Nest*, but with better intentions. Honestly, I felt so nervous about the nurse and about the forty to fifty stitches she said she would remove from my back that I told her Jen would do it, if she didn't mind.

Once I got back home, I had to explain to Will and Zoey about what happened and about how Daddy's back was sore. I told them they couldn't jump on Daddy like before. They respected my request. Sometimes I'd be sitting on the couch resting and one of them would come over and gently touch my back. They wanted to see it and wanted to go over it gently.

"Is Daddy hurt?" they would ask.

There's always that point in a parent's life when lifting the kids becomes harder and harder. When they're young and you want them to come over or go do something, one option you always will have is simply picking them up and bringing them over. But that certainly changed for me. For the first two months after surgery, I was pretty much useless. I used a walker for almost three weeks, then a cane for another two. I didn't go into the pet store for a month and a half, and couldn't drive for a month after returning home. When I finally did, I was still sore. I could feel every bump in the road. And for those of you who have been to Houston, you know that we are not short on our supply of potholes.

When something like this happens—where the improvement in your life is absolutely necessary, but you have to experience more pain before you come out the other side more capable—it's good to have family and friends helping out. Since Jen had to work, we were able to fly in family to stay with us and help out. I wasn't sure how things would turn out, but they ended up working out great. Initially, I flew back from my surgery at the Hospital for Special Surgery in New York with my father and had him stay for two nights, then my mom and step-dad came out and stayed for a week and a half, through Halloween. After that, my dad and step-mom came back to stay for a while.

I had to face reality, and that meant not being able to do certain things. I couldn't even go trick-or-treating (though I could eat the candy!). Picture a guy on pain medicine and miserable, barely able to walk around, opening the door as the kids shouted "Trick or . . ." They thought I was the trick. I walked like an angry zombie, lumbering slowly from the open door to the candy bowl and back for them to do the self-serve candy selection.

Imagine not being able to bend down or over or twist for anything. And I mean *anything*. This would include using the restroom. And without going into details on that particular area of my life, I did have a couple of months of being petrified and wondering whether I'd ever be able to do all the necessary things I needed to do myself.

I was smart enough to say no to one thing: filming more for the show. We had already filmed enough for the season, taking a break right after Halloween, but they asked if I wanted to continue to shoot anything more.

"Nah—we're good," I told them.

The world saw enough Bill Klein. They didn't need to see him suddenly going back to his potty-training days. That sort of nostalgia is what causes people to have nightmares.

The training that led to the injury with my back was a lesson in knowing my limits. Recovering from the surgery was a lesson in improving my life. I needed to be healthy for the sake of Jen and the kids. I needed to take care of myself, even if that meant having to take myself out of the game for a while in order to recover.

I've learned to take it easy. Workouts nowadays consist of most of the exercises I used to do. I've always had LPP, as Jen and I call them (Little People problems). So whatever LPP I used to have certainly didn't go away after surgery. Now, because of my spinal fusion and the hardware in my back, I literally can't bend. Though you're not supposed to bend your back while working out anyway.

A workout these days will include some light work on the rowing machine. I don't put my lower back into it but I do use my legs and arms for the cardio, and look to strengthen my back by finishing the row with a squeeze of my scapulae toward my spine.

I have a sixteen-inch mountain bike that I turned into a stationary bike in my exercise room. It's a kid's sixteen-inch Trek. I remember when those were so cool.

You can also find a blue yoga mat and a yellow exercise ball in the room. And last but not least, I have a one-seat universal gym that has everything I need—the lat pull, the bench press, pulldown bar, pulleys. A few other items litter the room—balance balls, dumbbells and barbells, and a bunch of autographed Giants gear that I have yet to properly display on the walls.

There is one thing you can't find: a kettle bell. I still try to improve my body and stay healthy, but now I do it slightly more reasonably.

SIMULATE IMPROVEMENTS

Jen

"You lose a crew, even in a simulation, and it's doom."

These words come from James Hannigan, the lunar module branch chief at Manned Spacecraft Center, later renamed Lyndon B. Johnson Space Center, in Houston, Texas. He worked there from 1962 to 1981. His team was an important part of helping a man land on the moon.

One thing Hannigan and his team knew about were simulations. Simulations are something I'm passionate about in my work at the Simulation Center at Texas Children's Hospital. At the Center, we re-create the high-risk scenarios we encounter in the real world every day, and use them to train doctors, nurses, and other health-care professionals to improve communication and teamwork, and ultimately patient care. We use highly technical mannequins, actors, real equipment, and real health-care providers to create a very realistic atmosphere—a simulation—similar to any number of actual situations that occur every day in a working hospital. After we execute the scenario, we move to a meeting room where we debrief the entire team on what occurred during the simulation, along with a detailed review of strengths, weaknesses, and areas needing improvement. In Hannigan's simulations, Apollo astronauts prepared for their missions by acting out—simulating—what they would do in any given situation. They would train for every possible moment and scenario related to their mission, from being inside the spacecraft, to encountering a problem outside the space module on the surface of the moon. Their goal was to be prepared for every situation that might come up. There was a very good reason for all this training. Do you remember what happened with Apollo 13? It was documented in the famous film by Ron Howard: The Apollo 13 mission had a fuel-cell tank explode that damaged the service module, leading to the familiar utterance, "Houston, we've had a problem."

Suddenly, the mission was no longer to land on the moon but to rescue the three astronauts, who were 200,000 miles away from Earth, and get them back home. NASA flight director Gene Kranz led the troop of flight controllers in trying to figure out every sort of feasible way to guide the men of Apollo 13 back home. This would include hundreds of different people—astronauts, engineers, and staff around the world. All of them would take each problem and try to solve it.

In the movie, Kranz delivers the famous line "Failure is *not* an option," and though he never stated that in real life, that was how he and the rest of NASA operated. And since the controllers and the astronauts had undergone countless simulations, nobody was going to suddenly make a rash decision without having the facts to understand what would happen. That's why they went to work on identifying and diagnosing every complication that arose.

Another great line from Kranz in the film applies to all walks of life:

"Let's *work* the problem, people. Let's not make things any worse by *guessing*."

As it turned out, simulations, and the preparation they led to, would end up being the thing that saved those pilots' lives. It actually wasn't simulations done by the crew of Apollo 13 that made a difference; rather, it was the ones that had been done a year earlier for the Apollo 10 flight that mattered. But in any case, instead of losing three astronauts and setting the U.S. space program back, the Apollo 13 crew was saved. It's a powerful story of heroism and bravery and intelligence. It's also a wonderful example of why simulation is a good thing, and how it can help save lives.

As the medical director of the Simulation Center at Texas Children's Hospital, it's a given that I'm going to talk about the need for simulation. And it's easy to point to a movie like *Apollo 13* as an example of why it's important. Even Jim Lovell (played by Tom Hanks) says it himself when NASA informs him they have to replace one of his crew before the mission: "He's a fine pilot, but when was the last time he was in a simulator?"

Wouldn't that make a great T-shirt for our Simulation Center? WHEN WAS THE LAST TIME HE WAS IN A SIMULATOR? Perhaps I'll have to inquire with the makers of the film on permissions for that.

Sarcasm aside, I do believe that simulation training has never been more important than it is today. To be leading the charge to use simulation to improve health care at Texas Children's is exciting. I love the place and the team of talented professionals I'm working with. Our state-of-the-art facility hosts many different health-care professionals who come there to train, observe, and then debrief for real-life pediatric and obstetric crises.

Simulation is all about improving. We bring in doctors, nurses, respiratory therapists, and child life specialists to help them train for whatever might come up in their jobs. They're all practicing clinicians and have already finished school or are professionals in their respective fields. Going to a simulation center, where they get to act out what they would do in an emergency, allows them to put themselves on the edge of their comfort zone and improve.

The reality of today is that health-care knowledge and complexity have exceeded our individual abilities and capabilities. Over the years, statistics have shown that seventy percent of the mistakes made in medicine are a result of errors in how clinicians work together as a team, how they communicate in a crisis. Teamwork problems and miscommunication, not a lack of knowledge or skills on behalf of the clinicians, are often the problem.

The goal in simulation is to create scenarios where the providers can make these mistakes in a safe environment, discuss, reflect, and learn from them in debriefing, with the ultimate goal of learning how to prevent those mistakes from happening in the real world.

When I was applying to medical school, I never could have realized that my career path would end up in health-care simulation, focusing on education and patient safety. I had always been drawn to education and even received awards as a junior educator early on in my medical training. What I love about simulation is that it is the only type of education where clinicians can actually practice and learn from their errors in communication and teamwork.

Someone like Dr. Kopits was a cowboy. And we definitely need them. But now more than ever we need teams to work together as a crew. We have to think of hospitals as kind of a pit crew, with multiple subspecialists all caring for one patient. Simulation is a way of training together. It's working together in either a formal simulation, or just practicing to help us get used to being together.

If we don't continue to improve, we will make more mistakes. This not only applies in health care, but in all aspects of life. It's important to try to implement ways to improve in whatever you're involved with.

As the movie *Apollo 13* shows us, practice alone doesn't make things perfect, but it can help us know how to react when life shows us its imperfections. In any field, or really with anything in life, the key is to practice, with constant improvement. And when you think you've got it down perfectly, keep practicing. There's always room for improvement.

Obviously for astronauts and doctors, that's easy to understand, but what about for others? How can you apply that idea to your own life, whether you're a retired grandmother or a teenager or in business for yourself or trying to potty-train your toddler?

First, you could think through all the different ways you could approach a given situation. Then, you could decide what makes the most sense given what you know. You might rehearse, either in your head or out loud, the words you might use or the actions you might take depending on how things play out. You could practice responding to various outcomes.

Then, you keep going, and you make it a priority to keep going. If you're learning how to play the piano, you have to spend time practicing. You can do this with a teacher at predetermined times, but it's up to you how often you do it on your own. For potty training with your child, you can work through whatever method you are going to use to train them ahead of time, but then once you start, you have to be consistent and keep at it.

Writing a book, for instance, is not something you sit down and do in one evening. Writers will usually spend years honing their craft. The writing itself can be a form of training and exercise. You can be testing out your voice and style, and each paragraph and page can be a simulation of sorts, until you're working on a project and you're lost in your own creative space, toiling until the final page is done. Even then, when you think you've written "The End," it isn't always the end. More improvements can be found. Right up until the book goes to press! Present paper included.

Life doesn't always give you ways to simulate your circumstances in order to improve. There's not a training that allows you to imitate what it's like to be married, for instance. Unless you have had five spouses before, you can never know what to fully expect, since humans are not machines. (Though at that point you might start to wonder if it's your behavior that needs to improve!) There's no simulation for becoming a parent. No cat, dog, or dozen eggs will provide the training or confidence you want to have before starting a family. Yet we can try to improve ourselves and to be ready for life-changing situations.

Life doesn't usually drastically change for us every day. And that's a good thing. After a crazy few years, I'm grateful that Bill and I haven't recently had to call home to say, "Houston, we've had a problem." Thankfully, there have been very few explosions, and those have usually only been explosions of toys around our house.

Improvement comes from not only trying new things, but also from repeating tasks, practicing so you can get better. We can only grow by learning, and one very effective way you learn is by doing something over and over again. As the ancient Latin phrase goes, *Repetitio est mater studiorum or* . . . Repetition is the mother of all study/learning.

KEEP ON IMPROVING

Bill

Most people know I'm a car aficionado. Some might call it a hobby or an interest. Others might say it's an obsession. I've just always loved vehicles and have constantly been trying to improve each subsequent car I drive. I like to think this is a great metaphor for life—how we should continually strive to keep building and growing.

So here is Bill Klein's Twelve-Point Plan toward improving your life. It's a carefully calculated chronology of my car collection that celebrates growth. Consider this a book-within-a-book, a road map, if you will, the ways in which I have constantly sought improvement.

1. **Start Here**

My mom was nice enough to give me my first car: a 1987 Dodge Omni, affectionately named the Eggmobile, a.k.a. Eggy. It was silver with a gray cloth and pleather interior. That's no typo—it was *pleather*. The radio was decent. It had a 2.2-liter 4-cylinder engine. It did zero 0 to 60, eventually. The front-wheel drive made my Omni a reasonably fun car to drive, if you liberally applied the emergency brake when cornering. But it was a bit of a lemon. And after a short time with me behind the wheel, it began to fall apart. It had a carburetor and the set screw for fuel/air mixture kept falling out, so I would sometimes need to rev up the engine at a traffic light just to prevent it from stalling. Old ladies I'd pull up next to at a light would think I was revving the engine to encourage a race. Then they would punch it and leave me in the dust.

Everyone has to start somewhere. Your starting point might be that awkward little kid you used to be, or the first day of the new year, when you're finally going to get your act together. Whatever your goal is, this is where you begin.

My Omni was not a bad starter car. It did its job—until it didn't. The coroner's report for that car stated death by neutral drop while going 40 backward down a hill. When you're just starting out, you're going to test limits sometimes, right?

Perhaps this can be read as a lesson about doing too much too soon. Or perhaps it's a lesson in not being stupid. Either way, you're learning.

2. Shaky Progress

My next car was a 1981 Chevy Monte Carlo.

With a name like Monte Carlo, how could you go wrong? It sounds exotic and European and opulent and daring. But no. It was a Chevy.

The Monte Carlo was light blue with a faded blue hood and snow tires in the rear. This car had a V-6 that had something called blow by. It wasn't a factory option, but rather a problem with the car. For some reason, the previous owner drilled a hole in the valve cover and put a hose from it back into the air filter intake where the carburetor was. It would spit oil into the filter and then back into the engine, where it would burn and produce a cloud of smoke. This happened mostly when the engine was hot.

After the coroner's report on this car I sold it to a coworker/janitor. His dad paid me the same amount I bought the car for a year earlier, so right away I had done well since it hadn't depreciated. The kid who drove it ended up wrapping it around a pole. He was fine. The car . . . not so much.

So lesson of car number 2: What seems like an improvement might actually be you getting into more than you bargained for. Or the lesson could be to replace the snow tires before you crash into a pole.

3. Settling for Something

Next came a maroon 1987 Pontiac 6000SE wagon.

I say wagon, but let's be honest—it's a station wagon.

I'll also be honest in telling you it was another hand-me-down, this time generously extended by my dad and stepmom. This car was a boat.

The Pontiac 6000SE was a lot like the Thanksgiving and Christmas holidays right after you decided to go on a diet. I put a lot of miles on it, and they were hard miles. They weren't pretty miles. The maroon microfiber interior was pretty awful, but that car did get me to countless interviews and, eventually, was my commuter for a number of months into my first career.

4. Start Anew

There's nothing wrong with suddenly wiping the slate clean and starting over. With *anything*. Yes, this is *The Curious Case of Bill Klein's Car Collection* I'm sharing here, but this advice can definitely apply to any self or home or life or soul makeover. You get to a point and then you realize, *That's it, let's start again.*

So you buy something new.

Like a 1997 Chevy Cavalier.

This would be my first new car. I leased it and proceeded to commute thirty miles each way to work for three years. It was a good little car. It did its job and was reliable. Sure, I got a lot of flack for its metallic teal paint and pinkish purple Rally Sport lettering on each side. I understood how it could be the butt of many jokes.

But to me, it was an improvement. I was no longer driving something that smoked or broke down. It was steady and stable. As you get older, you realize that pink lettering isn't as big of a deal as stability.

The Chevy Cavalier and I eventually got rear-ended at a traffic light by a kid going 50 mph at impact. My brother was in the car with me, and thankfully we both walked away from the crash. Needless to say, I got rid of that car instead of buying out the lease, and with 54,000 miles on the odometer, I was implored to lease another Chevy.

5. Celebrate Firsts of Any Kind

That brings me to my fifth car.

A 2000 Chevy Malibu.

So here's the thing. It performed well, and had a bigger motor than my previous car. It had four doors and front-wheel drive. The gray leather inside was actual leather (at least some of it), and this was a first for me.

In hindsight, I will admit that the Malibu's rear spoiler was the only thing about that car that didn't say geek. But the black exterior and wheels instead of hubcaps helped to keep the jokes from pouring in.

Little by little, my cars were improving.

6. You Find True Love

Yes, it can happen. You can get to a point where you finally are sitting there realizing something.

I love this.

After a whole lot of getting by and then settling for something else and feeling fine, you can wake up and feel a thrill. This is what happened when I drove my next car for the first time.

It was a 2003 Infiniti G35 coupe.

Let me go into alpha car mode on you. It had 280 hp, 270 ft-lb torque, a GPS, paddle shifters, red exterior, and a black interior. And if you don't understand what some of this means, all I will tell you is it all adds up to AWESOMENESS.

I used to sit in that car just to listen to it idle. (Maybe this was why I didn't have a very active love life.)

It was fast, too. So yes, red may not have been a good color for me. I was still in my twenties (for another year or so) and still had a lead foot, so I got a few speeding tickets. My only accident that was my fault happened in this car, too. It was October 18, 2004. I had just received news that my office and its staff would be laid off from their jobs. I was driving home, thinking about how I would handle this uncomfortable situation with the twenty-plus employees I had working for me. While in the midst of stop-and-go traffic, my mind was wandering and I forgot the whole stop part. Of course, the old man in front of me jammed on his brakes, so . . .

7. You Settle In

I was becoming older and wiser, but that didn't mean I wanted to be boring. I was ready for a little more strength and sophistication. So I got myself a 2006 Infiniti G37 in silver.

Six months prior to my lease ending with the G35 coupe, Infiniti called me to see if I wanted a new lease. They gave me one of those offers I couldn't refuse: a special deal that would be just twelve months long and would reduce my payment with nothing out of pocket.

So hello, G37.

Sometimes our journeys can take us in a new and unexpected direction. One success can bring another, and it can bring it quickly. Do you stay put and settle and play it safe? Some do. But if it makes sense, why not take another step up the stairway of life? That's exactly what I did.

One example of this for Jen and me would be discovering we would be able to adopt Will, then right away realizing we could adopt Zoey as well. We didn't play it safe—no way. If we had, we would have missed out on a whole universe of amazing that Zoey brought into our lives.

So back to my seventh car. I beat the snot out of the G37 for eleven months. It was the same car as the G35 but with more horsepower and a little more elegance. And since it was silver, I didn't get pulled over nearly as often. At the end of the lease, I returned to Infiniti, where they convinced me to get one more.

8. You Keep What Works (and You Keep It Growing)

So my next car:

The 2008 Infiniti G37S.

This one had new lights and bigger flares on the body. It had more horsepower at 330 and it came in all black. Even the exhaust note was a bit cooler.

My G37S is an example of what they call staying the course. Sticking with what works. My Infinitis had all been amazing cars, and this was just another step up. It wasn't drastic, but not all changes in life are. In fact, most changes in life and in us happen little by little.

I drove this car to Texas as Jen and I migrated south to Houston. The windows happened to be down a lot during that trip. And a ticket or two may have been paid.

As it turned out, Houston was a much better town to drive a sports car around in. So I needed to adjust in the only way that seemed fitting when it came to the whole idea of improving.

9. Change Can Be Good, or It Can Be *Spectacular*

Once I realized what the weather in Houston was like, I convinced Jen that a convertible would be the best new car for me. Sure, she didn't take too much convincing. We both knew I love cars. And because of that, I decided to take it up a notch with the following:

The BMW M3.

If you were into working out, this car would be like checking out your six-pack abs. If you excelled at business, this car would be like checking out your monthly sales report. The M3 is the sudden realization that all your hard work has paid off. Or in my case, all those cars (including those first few crappy ones) led up to this amazing one.

The 2011 M3 had 414 hp and went from 0 to 60 in 4.5 seconds. It was a hardtop convertible with a black exterior and a tan leather interior. *Real* leather, of course. It had GPS, paddle shifters, a dual-clutch transmission, an incredible sound system, big wheels. It was fast and loud and absolutely fun.

Yes, it was a step up. I finally bought a car with that iconic blue-and-white propeller on the hood . . . and it was reflected in the sticker price.

Yet it was worth every penny.

I'm proud and ashamed at the same time when I admit I've driven every car I've owned to its maximum speed limit. The Omni topped out around 90 to 95 (downhill with a tailwind); the Monte Carlo could do about 110; the wagon around 100 (yes, it's a station wagon doing 100); the Cavalier around 110; the Malibu about 110.

Kids, I'm not encouraging this at home. And just to let you know, no woodland creatures met their demise while I was driving my cars to their limits.

The Infinitis and M3 were limited by a governor to a mere 155 miles an hour, a speed I have verified. Of course, the M3 got there a lot quicker than the rest.

10. You Grow Up

I realize you can't be twenty-four all your life. You can't drive a convertible and dream about getting it up to 155 miles an hour. Eventually, you have to move on. Perhaps this is when you decide to take it easy. Maybe it's when responsibilities tell you to be more responsible. It could be when your family suddenly goes from two to four in a few blinks. That's when you might decide it's time for a change.

Change is good. Well, it is unless you lose your mind and decide to suddenly go back to driving an '87 Pontiac 6000SE wagon.

I bought Jen an Audi when we first started dating. It was an A4 Quattro. She was driving a real piece of . . . work. The aforementioned KIA Sportage circa 1996. It was breaking down a lot, so I decided to spend a little and get her something reliable. Something that would make her shout *"Was ist das?"* The Germans know their cars, as Jen would come to realize.

Subsequent to that one, we got Jen a new model they introduced, the Q5. When that lease was up, we got her another one. And since we had adopted Audis into our family now, getting one for myself seemed right. They kept giving me good deals and I liked the reliability and interiors. So shortly after we brought Will home, I decided I, too, needed a "family friendly" car. We all need to eventually grow up and get the family car, right?

Go ahead, minivan . . . Make my day.

Yeah, right.

That's the thing with improving and growing and changing in life. You can decide to do the responsible thing, but nobody should dictate *how* you do this. I had made a vow that no minivan would ever be in my driveway unless it belonged to someone else. So I went to Audi and they had a very nice S7 sedan with a hatch. I could easily justify this purchase. It just seemed so practical and logical for a father of two.

It was kind of like my old Dodge Omni but with an engine triple the size.

The Audi had seating for four, which was perfect since we knew Zoey was coming home soon. It had lots of room in the back for a double stroller, groceries, and other junk. It also came with 420 hp, 406 ft-lb torque, 0 to 60 in 4.4 seconds, all-wheel drive, and a dual-clutch transmission.

Daddy's home.

11. **Keep Making Improvements. Always.**

Most recently, I did a refresh of my 2014 S7. Audi ended up putting me in a black 2016 S7 with 450 hp, some added bells and whistles, and . . . something special: a very cool interior . . . drool.

I don't need to tell you that it's quite a bit of an upgrade and an improvement going from a 1987 Dodge Omni to a 2016 Audi S7. But it didn't happen overnight. You usually don't win *American Idol* nor do you win the $1.5 billion Powerball.

Improvements can take time. They can take many years—decades, even. And there can be a lot of starts and stops between where you began and where you end up. While you're living your life day to day, it's hard to see the progress you're making. It's only when you get far enough along that you can look back and realize how far you've come.

Your Dodge Omni has become an Audi S7.

12. **Keep the Dream Alive**

So what happens when you meet your goal, when you reach that pinnacle in whatever area you're growing and improving?

You continue to climb and to hope and to improve.

I dream about someday owning a classic Porsche 356, 911 Turbo S, or the all-new GT3 RS. Or a Ferrari 458 Italia with the cool stripes. Or a . . . well, a guy can dream.

"Come on, Bill. You shouldn't be doing this to yourself. Those are just s****y pipe dreams."

Aw, why don't you shut it, Morgan?

Of course, I have lots of other goals in my life. Cars are indeed a fun hobby and something I truly love. But I know I'd go back to that Dodge Omni in a heartbeat if I had to choose between my dream car and improving something in the lives of Jen or Will or Zoey. A car is just a car.

Unless it's the Porsche 356.

In this case, cars are just examples I'm using of stages in a journey. You might be able to make a similar list of your progress for something you love: A career, perhaps. A business. A talent. Even a relationship . . . with your car.

I'm not telling you that everything in life should be an upgrade. Or that it *will* be an upgrade. But what I am encouraging you to see is how that Dodge Omni can become an Audi S7. Through growing up and working hard and growing a business and turning one investment into another, little by little, progress is made.

Maybe you're wanting to make an improvement to an aspect of your life. Perhaps you're stuck in the same old same old. Maybe you're adjusting to the upgrade you just made.

Wherever you might be in whatever journey you're on, my encouragement to you is to never slow down. To keep going. To keep trying out new vehicles. To not be afraid of sticking with one you love. And in the same mind-set, to not be afraid of improving on something you already dearly love.

NEVER STOP IMPROVING

Jen and Bill

You might not have reached the pinnacle of success in your field yet. Your plan to start a family might be off to a rocky start. You might not be in the best shape of your life. And you might not be driving the car you saw on the cover of *Car and Driver* while at the grocery store, and we haven't gotten there yet, either. But the cool part is none of that matters. Our encouragement to you is the same thing we tell ourselves all the time: The story is never over. Every day is a chance to become better at something and to improve.

Every day gives you the opportunity to ask yourself this question:

What's something I can improve in the world?

It can be anything. Your personal life as a parent or a spouse. Something in your profession. Perhaps it's something in the community around you that you'd like to change.

Each day there are opportunities to become better and to make progress. Even if you have achieved your dream—whether it's something fun like driving an incredible car or it's something meaningful like achieving your career goals—you have to remember to keep on improving.

Thinking Big means finding something you want to accomplish, whether it's at work or in your personal life, and not stopping until you have achieved those goals. Then, when you do that, you find new things you want to accomplish and you continue to progress and grow.

A THINK BIG AND IMPROVE BIBLIOGRAPHY

Books to help you improve in different areas of your life

The 7 Habits of Highly Effective People by Stephen R. Covey. A powerful book that helps people solve personal and professional problems.

The Five Love Languages by Dr. Gary Chapman. Ever wonder why the person you love is so different from you? Dr. Chapman explains five different love languages we each have: Words of Affirmation, Quality Time, Receiving Gifts, Acts of Service, and Physical Touch.

The Road Less Traveled by M. Scott Peck, MD. Dr. Peck opens the book with the famous line "Life is difficult" and then proceeds to share a journey about spiritual growth. Understanding ourselves is a hard and often painful process but rewarding at the same time.

The Year of Yes by Shonda Rimes. Shonda Rimes is the legendary creator of such life-changing shows as *Grey's Anatomy, Scandal,* and *How to Get Away with Murder.* She is known not only for creating gripping, engrossing hit television shows, but also for populating those shows with people of all shapes, sizes, and colors. In this book, she shares about how making a conscious decision to be open to new experiences—to saying yes to whatever she was invited to do—changed her life. Reading it might change yours as well.

Crucial Conversations by Kerry Patterson. This book is all about effective communication. A great read for managers in the workplace looking to take their conversational skills to the next level. It's just as helpful for discussions at home, with your spouse or your children.

Who Moved My Cheese? by Spencer Johnson. A good book about dealing with change.

How to Master the Art of Selling by Tom Hopkins. This book was given to me when I first started out in medical sales. Great tools for selling. Great lessons that extend well beyond a job.

Good to Great by Jim Collins. A book that examines why some companies succeed while others fail, but with some great takeaways for improving your own personal life.

The Gifts of Imperfection by Brene Brown. An intelligently written and inspiring book about ignoring labels, discovering self-worth, and being happy with being you.

CHAPTER EIGHT

GO FOR IT

"I can't imagine a person becoming a success who
doesn't give this game of life everything he's got."

—Walter Cronkite

GO AHEAD AND START FILMING

Bill

Jen and I took a leap of faith when we decided to go for it and begin our show, *The Little Couple*. The taping began in October 2008. As we've mentioned before, we felt it was a fantastic opportunity to introduce viewers to and educate them about what it means to be a Little Person. And you already know that we didn't have great expectations. We didn't think the show would perform any better than anything else. We knew how tough television could be based on how many shows we enjoyed in the past that didn't have the number of eyeballs necessary to stay on the air. So honestly, we half expected it to fail after the pilot. I remember watching it from my bedroom in the house in New York. We were selling the house since Jen had already moved to Houston and was working there. I was commuting back and forth to my offices in New York, and by this time, all the house had in it was my queen-sized bed, a TV with cable, Wi-Fi, and a couple of TV dinner trays. It was quite barren.

Since we hadn't seen the show before it aired, it was a strange sort of thing when it finally came on. My mom and step-dad had come over to watch it with us, bringing some Chinese food with them. At the very least we would be able to enjoy some General Tso's chicken that night. After every single commercial break, I would make the same sort of comment: "Well, that wasn't awful."

We were very critical of our appearance, what we said, and how we said it. Our expectations were low: We just wondered how horrible it would be. And it turned out to be pretty okay. It was fun, and they had done a good job editing it. My parents eventually left and then Jen and I went to bed.

Four hours later I'd be woken up by my own voice. I wasn't talking in my sleep. At least, not in the way we normally refer to. We had fallen asleep with the TV on and I had no idea TLC would end up rerunning the show at one in the morning. I climbed out from underneath my covers and saw myself talking on television. To say the least, it felt like I was in some sort of surreal dream.

It would turn out that going for it was a pretty good decision. The pilot ended up doing well, opening up with decent ratings. At the time we didn't know the difference between good and great numbers and how everything worked. We did know they must have been pleased enough when they encouraged us to go ahead and do more shows. Jen and I were in Texas at a car show when we heard the news from the production company. I was on crutches so Jen was driving. We had just gotten out of the car when the phone call came.

"You're not going to believe this," the producer said. "The show got picked up for a season—twelve episodes."

Once again, a surreal feeling suddenly came over me. We walked around a bit dazed and confused, laughing in disbelief that this was really happening.

What have we gotten ourselves into?

Going for it was one thing. Now we were diving into the deep waters.

We were assigned a new field producer and our second episode of television documented our migration from New York to Texas.

Just like everything in our lives, Jen and I have decided to take our journey with the show step by step and season by season. All along, there have never been any expectations. It's been fun and we've enjoyed the world out there getting to know us and our families, colleagues, and friends.

For the first few seasons of *The Little Couple*, it was basically a two-person show. We weren't the biggest show on the network, but we were chugging along with ratings that kept us a viable solution for the ten p.m. time slot on Tuesdays. But then something happened. As we settled into our lives in Houston and began our journey to start a family, our show did something not all shows do. Our life story began to change. Not intentionally, but naturally.

With the fertility struggles and then the journey with adoption, existing viewers stuck around, and a new audience of couples, families, and kids began to watch. The show was no longer just about educating the world about people with differences overcoming obstacles; it was now about different people overcoming obstacles all too familiar to the viewer at home. The spotlight really did shift in some ways from our stature. Now it was about experiencing the highs and lows of life: fertility treatments and miscarriages and adoption and cancer and surgery and family growth.

Once Will and Zoey entered our lives, the audience instantly fell in love, too. How could they not? Have you seen how adorable they are? We have been able to keep a balance so far. We haven't changed who we are or what we do. We still work hard every day, still put our kids to bed every night and cook them breakfast every morning. We are big on little projects. We are an avid reading family too. Every night we read at least one book together as a family. We do playtime in, out, and around the house. We even try to teach them sports. We are the typical soccer parents . . . hauling the kids to events on the weekends. We do our best to be good examples for Will and Zoey and we are always working to keep a normal life outside of the world of television.

It's been strange at times. Like having some random viewer come to our front door on Christmas Eve at ten p.m. wanting to talk and share a glass of wine with us. We're all about being hospitable, but late at night on Christmas Eve is a whole other story. One Sunday morning while I was taking out the trash, I noticed there was a woman standing across the street from our house taking pictures. You could tell she was from out of town because her eyeglass frames were neon green . . . definitely a more trendy European style. I had to go over to the woman to see what she was doing. She told me she was a huge fan and wanted to show her family back home where she'd been. So we took a selfie on my front lawn. Sometimes, the timing is right to say hi . . . and sometimes the only stranger entering my house on Christmas Eve should be Santa Claus.

We don't view the show as our job, but as a very time-consuming hobby. We are seemingly unique in that, aside from a few more people in attendance, much of what we do with cameras present is what we do, and have been doing, without cameras. And that is very convenient, especially since our acting skills leave something to be desired. We have been able to live our lives unscripted, and so far, it's done a lot of what we had hoped it would do.

People have often asked me what my favorite episodes have been. I always say it's the stuff that happens in the hospital, the stuff I could never have seen otherwise. It's when Jen is in her job and living her professional life. She might be in the NICU or making a presentation to the board and it's amazing to see her. I just watch her and think, *That's my wife!* And as I said, I would never have been able to see this if it wasn't for the show. The hospital doesn't exactly have a "Bring Your Idiot Husband to the NICU" day.

As always, when it comes to thinking about the future of our show, we continue to play it by ear. We let Will and Zoey decide what they want to do with their time. That is, when they don't have school or any of their extracurricular activities. Sometimes they are very happy to have the crew around and a television show is born.

Other times they are not in the mood and B roll of the city of Houston is born. (That's a television show joke.)

We're just happy that our viewership loves our kids. We're grateful. But there are many aspects of our kids' lives that aren't seen on the show, and that's by choice.

We have to laugh and have fun. That's how we approach it. If it goes away tomorrow, that's okay. If it continues to go for a bit longer, and as long as it continues to provide a positive message to the world at large—awesome.

Who would have imagined that all of this would come out of an invitation for Jen to be on a morning news show? As you know, we said no at first. But eventually, we decided to say, "Let's go for it."

That's how we've always lived our lives, and that's how we will continue to live them. Being willing to give things a try.

ENCOURAGE OTHERS TO GO FOR IT

Jen

No amount of fear or heartache or hurt will ever compare to seeing the things your child faces. Bill and I have been blessed to discover that we no longer have to simply Think Big ourselves. Now we are given this great responsibility to raise our children and teach them to know and believe the same things we do, because we know for certain that challenges will arise for our kids. Will and Zoey are already starting to face some of the same issues we did when we were young. And we can't just read them our book and say, "See, we know what you're going through—we dealt with the same thing."

Our children will need to figure out how to go for it in their own ways. All we can do is encourage them and love them and continue to tell them not to be afraid, like we did recently when we encouraged Will to play soccer.

We knew what to expect, or at least some of the things to expect. Will was five years old, so basically he would be running around the field trying to get the ball in the goal somehow. We knew he wasn't likely to be diving for goals and heading his way to victory on his first go at it. But we hoped he would have fun and learn something. Still, Bill and I didn't want to torture him. We said that if he didn't like it, he didn't have to come back. But Will needed to experience enough of the sport in order to make a decision.

On his first day of practice, we knew what the decision would be. He wore one of the league's soccer T-shirts that was way too big for him. The field they were playing on hadn't been cut, so the grass was up to his knees. He had to run around a field with weeds and dandelions and we could just tell the poor guy was not happy.

By day three, he was miserable and just going through the motions. He would occasionally kick the ball, but the reality was most of the other kids had already played soccer. And Will's experience with soccer was very limited. His parents didn't play soccer. His sister didn't play soccer either. We quickly learned that he didn't love the sport and quite possibly never would. Yet we wanted to show him how to at least give it a shot, to at least try.

So Will tried and gave it a good shot. He went for it. And that was enough for us.

Even at Zoey's young age, we're still trying to instill in her the courage to go for things. For her, it's been more about socializing and engaging. Zoey has gears that are running constantly, and we've seen that from the moment we met her in India. We could see that Zoey immediately evaluates everything, and takes a cautious stance before she is willing to dive into anything.

One area we've told her to go for it is in the area of getting her to speak up, especially when people treat her like a baby. She used to let it happen, but then later would tell us she didn't like it when she was treated like an infant by her peers, like people picking her up just like they did their baby brother or sister, or patted her on the head. She hated this, but wasn't sure what to do. So we encouraged her to tell people that she didn't like them doing this. We helped give her the tools to tell people to stop (or eventually tell a grown-up).

Zoey entered her class at school younger than most. The kids in her class normally start at age three, but they made an exception for Zoey and let her in before her third birthday. So she was already one of the youngest, and then she was much smaller than anyone else in the class, too. That's not to say she hasn't made progress since we first met her and brought her home. She's gained more than fifty percent of her former body weight and now she's in the twenty-fifth to fiftieth percentile for children her age with achondroplasia, the type of skeletal dysplasia she was diagnosed with. She has grown by leaps and bounds in so many ways.

Our daughter is one tough cookie, and she stands up for herself. But she's only four years old now. So we're helping to instruct her with simple life lessons: If you don't like what someone does to you, let them know. Be polite but stern. Of course, we've had to explain what stern means to her. It doesn't mean giving someone the look of death or shutting down on them. There is something in between allowing others to take advantage of you and entering a staring contest with them . . . something hard to understand sometimes when you're four. She will master it, of that I have no doubt, with a little more time.

Parenting—what an adventure it can be. I look forward to all the moments where Will and Zoey will go for their dreams. After everything I've spent years learning as a neonatologist, I am still fascinated to find how much I learn from Will and Zoey and from how I relate to them as their mom. I won't ever forget seeing pictures of Will and Zoey for the first time and about suddenly being full of hope about the possibility of adopting them. Nor will I ever forget holding Will and Zoey in my arms for the first time.

"Go for it" isn't some sort of slogan for an advertisement for Bill and me. It's something we have always tried to live by. There are so many times where we had to make a choice to either go for it or risk watching our dreams pass us by. Deciding to get on DateA Little.com one fateful night and also moving ahead with the adoption process in a time of much loss both came from the decision to go for it. If either of us had been afraid to go for it then . . . Well, I don't want to think about the potential outcome.

We hope and trust we'll see our children learn to go for what they want in life. It doesn't matter to me what professions they choose, who they fall in love with, or what dreams they chase as long as they go for what they want in life with vigor, determination, and courage. I can't wait to hear them come to us one day to announce a big life-changing decision. I can't wait to see them face some sort of choice to go ahead and go for it. As long as we can keep on encouraging them and nudging them forward, regardless of the obstacle, we know they will find the strength and courage to realize that going for it can be a good thing.

GOING AND GOING BUT NEVER GONE

Bill

"So tell me a little about yourself."

This is a question you and I hear all the time. Every day we're invited to share who we are with people, whether it's new customers in the store or strangers off the street or someone on a social network. And when I ask other people similar questions, I've noticed something about how people define themselves. Most of the time when someone is asked to share who he or she is, they start with their profession.

"I'm a business owner," I might tell someone.

People will give themselves all sorts of definitions and labels: lawyer, doctor, accountant, barfly. It's easy for people to define themselves and others with what they do. I'm no different. I'll do this, too. Yet calling myself a businessman or even an entrepreneur still doesn't seem to really sum me up. I'm really diverse, with many interests. I like the creative side of education and doing things. I love inventing things. There is so much more to a person than superficial labels can capture.

In both of our books, I've shared parts of my journeys. From the medical side of life (which was a huge part of growing up) to college and then building a career, I've shown how certain passions and lots of persistence have paid off. So in the mind-set of continuing to think of ways to improve myself, and in the spirit of going for it, I'll tell you a bit about how I feel about where I am now.

I feel like, in many ways, I'm still just starting to reach some of my goals. I look around and feel that I have a lot to offer. Of course, your goals change as you get older and realize what's important—building a business doesn't compare to the gift of raising two amazing children. Yet I still have some hopes and dreams as I look ahead.

There are the inventions in the works, different things I have up my sleeve that I can't talk about yet. Creative ideas I've helped to shape and build and hopefully will launch one day.

Being in television has helped me learn a lot about the industry. I've always loved films and would love to write a screenplay or be involved in the background on some film.

I've loved being able to show a little of my humor on our show. I think comedians are heroes that bring levity to our world. Humor is a much-needed tool to overcome situations, one I've relied on my whole life. Comedy is one of the things I enjoy. I love to make people laugh. I'd love to continue to try stand-up in comedy clubs, along with writing comedy skits.

I dream of one day being involved with designing some type of car. I certainly know enough about them. How cool would it be to be involved with a project that takes something like a car to the next level? I'm fascinated by the marriage of performance and efficiency. So yes, I have the spirit of the driver, especially since I've been driving since I was eight. That's the only way I've ever gone fast. I realize I won't ever be a race car driver, but what if I owned a fraction of a Formula One race team? Just to be involved in racing and cars would be enough since it's my passion.

And what about football, another passion? That's another world I've thought about entering and going for in some type of capacity. Especially after my back surgery, when I met the former punter for the Giants Steve Weatherford. The NFL player regularly goes to the hospital to visit kids. One day he came in wearing a Superman costume and showed off his Super Bowl rings. While he was there, someone told him about this chubby forty-one-year-old Giants fan.

So there I was in the ICU after having lost a lot of blood. I had been getting a blood transfusion for twenty-four hours when Steve showed up. Ah, yes, such a great time to meet one of your heroes. I was swollen and miserably uncomfortable. But he was such an incredible man to take time out of his busy schedule to see sick kids (and adults) in the hospital. I've been able to keep in touch with him; we've even become Twitter buddies. His family watches our show. And after seeing what he does to inspire young kids, I've started thinking how much I'd like to continue to amplify my participation in speaking to kids who could use some inspiration. Or maybe someday I'll get a chance to infuse the Giants team with some words of inspiration. We all know they could use some after three consecutive years of missing the playoffs!

I've never been at a better place in my life to go for it. I have a long list of things I'd love to try. And I share those as examples of the way you should think, regardless of where you are in life. Make a list, perhaps yearly, spelling out things you would love to go for. Even if they're a bit outrageous, that's okay. You never know.

I'll watch an episode of our show and sometimes I'll have the same sort of out-of-body experience that I had when my own voice woke me up the night our first episode aired. I'll suddenly see our family doing something and it will strike me.

How'd I get here?

I will see Jen's beautiful smile and Will's never-ending joy and Zoey enthusiastically hopping and skipping along and just think, *When did I win the Powerball of life?*

Watching Jen with her patients and colleagues fills me with such pride. I know she's always worked hard and studied harder and did more to get the same acknowledgments. But everything she does isn't just due to her skill; it's because of her passion. And now to see her interacting with our children? It's incredible.

I'll see Will who is happy 99.9 percent of the time. The kid wakes up happy, goes to bed happy, reads a book feeling happy, takes a bath being happy, eats dinner happy, goes to school happy. It's crazy. It's crazy that I get to be his dad.

Then I look at the most beautiful, brilliant four-year-old in the world and catch her gaze. The fiery little one who used to refuse to lock eyes with me. Now she'll do it fondly. She has memorized most of the books on her bookshelf . . . a memory not so different from dear old dad. It's extraordinary. Extraordinary that she's my daughter.

I know that the incredible and crazy and extraordinary love that I've found came after I had decided to go for it. I don't applaud myself, but rather thank God. As I've said with the good and the bad that's come my way, God doesn't make mistakes.

Jen and I have been able to tell our story, and we're continuing to do it to this day. For that, we're grateful. We're glad to have people appreciating us for who we are. For people to see us and know that despite our stature we've been able to do X and Y and Z. That's always been important to us. Being different shouldn't be the defining characteristic of anybody. And if our program helps make the road a bit smoother for the next person to travel down it, even better.

Life is indeed short. And we do indeed encourage you to Think Big. Life has been this incredible and crazy and extraordinary road full of wonderful surprises. Three of them greet me every day. All I can hope to do is share the love in whatever way I can.

GO OUT AND GIVE BACK

Jen

My favorite marine biologist and underwater explorer once said: "When one man, for whatever reason, has the opportunity to lead an extraordinary life, he has no right to keep it to himself."

Jacques Cousteau was right. If you do have opportunities, for whatever reason, you shouldn't keep them to yourself.

I look at my life and feel that I can say this. Some people might look at my life and see the hardships and the difficulties and only have a feeling of sympathy. But I choose to look back and think of how extraordinary it's been, and then I look ahead and figure out ways to share it with others. And I try not to just share my life experiences with others, but also share the hope, the strength, the happiness, and the love I've been fortunate to have come across during my life.

My mother and father refused to ever give up on me. Instead, they were great examples of what courage, love, and determination can do for a child growing up with complex medical needs. They had to be willing to go for it without much guarantee of the results, but they did so because of their bravery and dedication to doing what was best for their daughter. I am forever grateful that they did not let fear prevent them from pursuing what must have been some of the scariest and most difficult decisions as a parent. How could I not share with the world how amazing my parents were in raising me? Now that we are in similar shoes, seeing both Will and Zoey go through their first operations, we learned how much harder it is to be the parents of a patient. Bill and I are both trying to be as strong for Will and Zoey as our parents have been for us.

I see the happiness surrounding me every day, starting with my best friend and biggest fan, Bill, who I'm lucky enough to have as my husband. I see the happiness in Will, who, as Bill put it, just stays that way all day long. His attitude toward life is infectious and changes everyone around him. He has, I am told by countless people who have viewed our program, made them happier. Pretty remarkable for a five-year-old kid from Inner Mongolia. Zoey is only four years old, and while she is still catching up on the growth charts, her heart is gigantic and her spirit is powerful. And she continues to blossom. She will, one day, be a woman with strength, dignity, and the courage to accomplish anything.

And then, whenever I think of sharing my life and my story, I think of sharing the same hope and life lessons that Dr. Kopits shared with me. His talents and medical expertise and daring vision all paled in comparison to the great love he had for all his patients and for the hope he gave them day after day.

Hope. The best sort of surgery you can ever find.

I'd like to think Dr. Kopits would have liked this book and these life lessons. He could have added a lot of thoughts to each of them himself. In so many ways, he helped write some of these stories and passages. He helped inscribe a lot of the inspiration I've held in my heart. I will never stop being grateful to that man.

There was an interview with Dr. Kopits that sums up his view on how he dealt with all people with short stature. It's amazing that a man so tall could have thought so big and made such a lasting impression in the world of Little People. It's one of the many ironies of life. He once stated the following:

> If they dropped us on another planet where everybody was short, they'd think we were the weird ones. We just wanted to get across the idea that Little People are important as people—not more important, not less important than other people, but as important.

Bill and I have always had the same view. We're not more important than anybody else, but we're not less important, either. We simply matter like everybody else.

All of us have disabilities we carry with us, whether they are visible or not. And all of us wake up each day carrying our own responsibilities and looking at the day in different ways. We want to encourage you to embrace hope and to never stop trying. Thinking Big is the starting point. But then you have to go out there and do it.

And whatever you do, do it with as much love as you can.

GO FOR IT

Now it's time to write out your own Think Big list. So write out the following:

TRY

HOPE

INITIATE

NO

KNOW

BELIEVE

IMPROVE

GO FOR IT

Now think of one way you can accomplish each goal.

What are you going to **TRY** today?

What sort of **HOPE** will you embrace?

What are you going to **INITIATE**?

What is the biggest **NO** in your life?

What is the number one thing you **KNOW** about yourself?

What do you **BELIEVE** can truly happen?

How can you **IMPROVE** something in your life?

And now . . . when are you going to **GO FOR IT**?

ACKNOWLEDGMENTS

Thank you to all of the people who have inspired us to strive to be better people, especially, but not limited to . . .

Our wonderful children, William Ri Jin Klein and Zoey Nidhi Klein. You make us want to try harder, do more, and be better. You have and continue to bring joy into our lives.

Thank you to our parents and stepparents, David and Judy Arnold, Barbara and Chuck Croner, Bill and Debbie Klein. You have set the bar very high. We can only hope to be as good to our kids as you were to us.

To our brothers, stepbrothers, sisters-in-law, and fantastic nieces and nephews—Thomas, Christine, Riley, and Reagan Klein; Joseph, Karen, Dorinda, and Joseph T. W. Klein; David and Lisa Arnold; Jonathan, Debra, and Maddie Richman; and James and Kayla Richman. Thank you for the laughter, memorable moments, and wonderful time together. Sibling relationships like ours are rare.

Acknowledgments

To the greatest friends anyone has ever had in history of old friends . . . Lakshmi Reddy, David Daubel, Chetna Bhattacharyya, Andria Donohue, Rajiv and Manju Kulkarni, and Tara Kaheny—without you guys, we wouldn't be us.

Thank you to Kate Apffel for going through everything with us these past few years. Clearly, you should have read the fine print before signing up to be our nanny!

Thank you to those who have helped us reach new heights in our careers, namely Dr. Tad Foote, Mike Sperduti, Julie May, and Roger Armstrong. Without you, Jen would likely still be a brilliant doctor and Bill would be a very mediocre used-car salesman in Birmingham, Alabama.

Thank you to David Zaslov, Nancy Daniels and team Discovery/TLC, and Eric Schotz, Ed Horwitz, Ruth Rivin, and team LMNO for your continued support over the past seven years.

Thank you to the people who have helped make us proud Little People, especially Bobby Van Etten, Diane Hawes, Donna Buscemi, and the most fantastic physician we have ever had the pleasure of meeting, the late Dr. Steven Kopits.

And a special thanks to Travis Thrasher, Steve Ross at the Abrams Artists Agency, and Judith Curr, Beth Adams, and Jonathan Merkh at Simon & Schuster, without whom this book would not be possible.

ABOUT THE AUTHORS

Jennifer Arnold, MD, graduated from the University of Miami with dual degrees in biology and psychology before going on to complete her medical degree at Johns Hopkins School of Medicine in Baltimore, Maryland, in 2000. She is currently an attending neonatologist at Baylor College of Medicine and medical director of the Simulation Center at Texas Children's Hospital. Dr. Arnold is married to her best friend, Bill Klein. They live in Houston, Texas, and have adopted two wonderful children. Jennifer and Bill are the stars of TLC's *The Little Couple*.

Bill Klein grew up on Long Island, New York. After earning a degree in biology from NYU, Bill became an entrepreneur and inventor. Today, he plays an active role in every business he owns, including Candu Enterprises, where he and his wife, Jennifer, provide a variety of media-related services, including making appearances at schools and other institutions to aid in the campaign to stop bullying. Most recently, Bill created Rocky & Maggie's, a pet supply business named after the family dogs. Bill Klein is married to his best friend, Jennifer Arnold. They live in Houston, Texas, and have adopted two fantastic children. Bill and Jennifer are the stars of TLC's *The Little Couple*.

ALSO BY
Jennifer Arnold, MD, & Bill Klein

NEW YORK TIMES BESTSELLER

Life Is Short
(no pun intended)

*Love, Laughter, and Learning to
Enjoy Every Moment*

FROM THE STARS OF TLC'S *THE LITTLE COUPLE*
Jennifer Arnold, MD, & Bill Klein

Available wherever books are sold or at SimonandSchuster.com

HOWARD BOOKS
AN IMPRINT OF SIMON & SCHUSTER, INC.
A CBS COMPANY